ROTTEN PROD

The Bairds, c.1922, courtesy of Victoria Jeremijenko, Brisbane, only
daughter of Kathleen and granddaughter of James Baird

ROTTEN PROD

The Unlikely Career of Dongaree Baird

EMMET O'CONNOR

UNIVERSITY COLLEGE DUBLIN PRESS
PREAS CHOLÁISTE OLLSCOILE BHAILE ÁTHA CLIATH
2022

First published 2022
by University College Dublin Press
UCD Humanities Institute, Room H103,
Belfield,
Dublin 4

www.ucdpress.ie

ISBN 9781910820858

CIP data available from the British Library

The right of the author to be identified as the author of this work has been asserted by him

Typeset in Dublin by Gough Typesetting Limited
Text design by Lyn Davies
Printed in Glasgow on acid-free paper by Bell and Bain Printers,
303 Burnfield Road, Thornliebank, Glasgow G46 7UQ

Contents

	Acknowledgements	vii
	A note on James Baird in Australia	viii
	Abbreviations	ix
	Introduction	xi
1	In the Black Squad	1
2	The 44	20
3	The Dongarees	31
4	Belfast Confetti	41
5	Hellfast	59
6	Organiser	77
7	The Last Battles	83
	Epilogue: From the Black Squad to the Black Legend	96
	Notes	99
	Bibliography	115
	Index	123

Contents

Acknowledgements

James Baird has been a person of interest since I heard about him from veterans of the Waterford farm strikes. One admirer of his recalled, 'aye, I'd say he was an Orangeman', meaning of course that he thought he was a Protestant. The lazy confusion about the labels was refreshing in the troubled 1970s. In that carelessness lay one of the great achievements of the Republic.

How could one not be curious about how a man from the black squad ended up leading Waterford farm labourers? I am grateful to all those who helped to answer the puzzle: especially Seán Byers, Charles Callan, Alan Campbell, Chris Coates, Robert Corbett, John Cunningham, Terry Dunne, Pauline Gardiner, Nóirín Greene, Mary Hackett for the genealogy, the late John Halstead, John McIlroy, Francis King, Fidelma McCorry, Kieran Jack McGinley, Barry McLoughlin, Ida Milne, Kevin Murphy, Lilli Poulsen, Lucy Taksa, Richard Temple, Helga Woggon, and Pádraig Yeates; the staffs of the Ulster University libraries, Belfast Central and Newspaper Library, Derry Central Library, Derry City Archives, the Independent Order of Rechabites, Queensland, the Modern Records Centre, Warwick, the National Archives, Dublin, the National Archives, Kew, the National Library of Australia, the National Library, Dublin, the Noel Butlin Archives, the PRONI, UCD Archives, Waterford Municipal Library, and the Working Class Movement Library, Salford; and colleagues of the School of Arts and Humanities and Professor Ian Thatcher for subventing the research. As always, I am obliged to Colette, Deaglán, Laura, and Magda. And finally, I am most indebted to the ever-understanding Noelle Moran, Conor Graham and the team at UCD Press.

I ndíl cuimhne Déise (2003-19), brocaire is cara den scoth.

Emmet O'Connor,
1 May 2022

A note on James Baird in Australia

Victoria Jeremijenko, granddaughter of James Baird, kindly supplied the following information after the book had gone to print. James Baird found it impossible to secure work in Australia and supported his wife, Frances, who opened a boarding house. James found it distressing not to be able to support his family and continued to cite his occupation as 'boilermaker' in the Australian census. As a very young child, Victoria remembered him late in life as enjoying long walks, talking occasionally of working on the *Titanic*, and reliant on an oxygen mask in his final years. I am obliged to Victoria for these recollections and for family memorabilia.

Emmet O'Connor

Abbreviations

AEU	Amalgamated Engineering Union
ASCJ	Amalgamated Society of Carpenters and Joiners
ASE	Amalgamated Society of Engineers
BEW	Belfast Expelled Workers
BTUC	British Trades Union Congress
EWRC	Expelled Workers' Relief Committee
FEST	Federation of Engineering and Shipbuilding Trades
GSC	General Strike Committee
ILP	Independent Labour Party
IRA	Irish Republican Army
ITUC	Irish Trades Union Congress
ITGWU	Irish Transport and General Workers' Union
LRC	Labour Representation Committee
MP	Member of Parliament
NSFU	National Sailors' and Firemen's Union
NAUL	National Amalgamated Union of Labour
OBU	One Big Union
RIC	Royal Irish Constabulary
UK	United Kingdom
UULA	Ulster Unionist Labour Association
WFA	Waterford Farmers' Association

Archives and sources

BPP	British Parliamentary Papers
MRC	Modern Records Centre
NLI	National Library of Ireland
PRONI	Public Record Office of Northern Ireland
SIPTU	Services, Industrial, Professional and Technical Union
UCDA	University College, Dublin Archives
USBMISS	United Society of Boiler Makers and Iron and Steel Shipbuilders
WCML	Working Class Movement Library

BELFAST MUNICIPAL ELECTIONS.
15th JANUARY, 1920.

SHANKILL DIVISION.

VOTE FOR

Gordon, Kyle & M'Williams

DAWSON GORDON
SAM KYLE
HUBERT M'WILLIAMS

The Official Labour Candidates

NOTE:—The only Official Labour Candidates are those endorsed by the

BELFAST LABOUR PARTY.

Some of Baird's running mates in the Belfast Municipal elections, 1920. Sam Kyle and Dawson Gordon were elected.

ITGWU officials in Waterford for the ITUC in 1918. Baird would work with Cathal O'Shannon and Joe Metcalfe (front row, first and second from left), Thomas Foran (second row, third from left), William O'Brien (second row, fourth from left), Nicholas Phelan (fourth row, first from left), Thomas Dunne (fourth row, far right), and Denis Houston (back row, far right).

Introduction

a sober, intelligent, and strangely honest and
courageous spokesman for his class.
Jim Larkin on Baird, *Irish Worker*, 6 October 1923.

James Baird was one of that extraordinary cohort of agitators thrown up by
the wave of syndicalist unrest in Ireland between 1917 and 1923. Like most
of his colleagues, he rose without trace, and disappeared just as mysteriously.
Within a few years of his departure, it seemed incredible that he or his kind
could ever have existed in Ireland. The enigma is compounded by the fact
that since the growth of interest in Belfast labour history in the 1970s,
his name has frequently popped into the literature on the shorter hours
movement among engineering workers in 1918, the 44 hours strike in 1919,
the 1920 municipal elections – the highpoint of post-war Labour radicalism
in Belfast – the shipyard expulsions, and the first elections to the Northern
Ireland parliament in 1921 with no biographical explanation.[1] Nothing has
been written on his background and career to 1918, his engagement with
the National Sailors' and Firemen's Union or the Irish Self-Determination
League in 1921–2, or on his family or personal life, though he was married
with six children. In another strange instance of occlusion, Baird's first-
hand reports and observations on the workplace expulsions were given
prominence by Fr John Hassan in *Facts and Figures of the Belfast Pogroms,
1920–22*, which Hassan published under the pseudonym G. B. Kenna. The
exposé was to be issued by the fictional O'Connell Publishing Company
in Dublin as part of the Provisional Government's propaganda war on the
Unionist regime, but a change in Dublin's Northern policy in early August
1922, from working against the Belfast government to working with it,
led to *Facts and Figures* being regarded as so incendiary that the print-run
was almost entirely pulped. Just 18 copies survived, and were circulated
privately.[2] Baird then retreated into obscurity again until re-surfacing
in 1922–4 as an organiser in the south east with the Irish Transport and
General Workers' Union (ITGWU). After that, he vanished completely. A

hagiography of his more famous daughter avoided her father's turbulent life in Ireland.[3]

Baird's career as a Labour agitator is all the more remarkable in that it took him from one extremity of Ireland's industrial, social, and political spectrum to the other. From the north-east to the south-east was a big step. In Harland and Wolff, he toiled as an artisan with the 'black squad', the men who did the heavy iron work, in the biggest and most technically advanced industrial site in Ireland. Within three years, he would be organising agricultural labourers and county council roadmen in Carlow, Kilkenny, and Waterford. In the shipyard, he worked in an odd juxtaposition of Orangeism and militancy. There are those who bridle at the sectarian tag and dispute which label best describes the yardmen, but as Haire's recollections of Harland and Wolff in the 1940s and 50s illustrate, they both coexisted and had their own internal divisions:

> It wasn't all cheerfulness and unity among the mainly Protestant workforce. There were tensions between them and rivalry among the Orange members. They spoke of those who had a few degrees of the Order above them—and who never seemed to be made redundant when things became slack.
>
> The surprising thing was the number of radical Protestant workers that existed who didn't belong to the Orange Order, B Specials and Freemasonry.... Generally the vast majority of the shipyard Protestant workforce got along with the Catholic in their midst. Though declaring themselves British, they somehow seemed to have adopted the open Irishness of friendship. Turn up having forgotten your sandwiches (Piece), and they would share what they had with you, despite what you were. Of course as a Catholic you kept your opinions to yourself. The odd one who didn't usually found a .303 rifle round in their jacket with a note saying: *"This will be in you not on you."*
>
> That was the time to leave, for a hard core existed that even had the radical Protestant keeping his mouth shut.[4]

Haire also recalled the absolute importance of holding a union card. If the workforce was conservative and normally tolerant of religions and politics, the bedrock forces were trade unionism and loyalism.[5] The yards offered an ordered environment, in which everyone knew their place and the rules that went with it. In provincial Ireland, Baird was plunged into the very fluid conditions of Ireland during the slump, in the febrile atmosphere of civil war. A Presbyterian and a Rechabite, he was nearly elected to Dáil Éireann by the workers of Waterford in 1923. The transition from the 'black North' to a nascent state still shuddering from the effects of revolution at home and abroad, was one he was eager to embrace. His experiences in Belfast had alienated him completely, not just from Unionists, but from the amalgamateds, as the British-based unions were known euphemistically in Ireland.[6]

In the process he moved from one of Britain's oldest craft unions to the upstart and pointedly Irish ITGWU, founded by the maverick Big Jim Larkin in 1909. The Boilermakers had originated as the Society of Friendly Boilermakers to cater chiefly for men in railway workshops in Manchester in 1834. Members addressed each other formally as 'worthy brother'. Dublin members of the Society were reported to be meeting in 1836, though its first recorded Irish branch was the Good Samaritan Lodge established in Belfast in 1841. In 1845 the union was renamed the United Friendly Boiler Makers' Society. To stay independent of the recently formed Amalgamated Society of Engineers, Machinists, Smiths, Millwrights and Pattern Makers, soon to be known simply as the Amalgamated Society of Engineers (ASE), and to reflect its increasing presence in shipbuilding, the Society became the United Society of Boiler Makers and Iron Shipbuilders in 1852, and the United Society of Boiler Makers and Iron and Steel Shipbuilders in 1898.[7] When Baird joined, its head office was in Newcastle-on-Tyne, and it had 37,300 members throughout the United Kingdom (UK), and an imperial reach, with branches, or lodges as they were designated, in Malta, Gibraltar, and South Africa. The general secretary assured the Royal Commission on Labour in 1893 that his executive avoided strikes and had accumulated a reserve fund of £190,000. The vast bulk of its annual spending was on sickness, accident, out-of-work, superannuation, and charitable benefits.[8]

The contrast with the syndicalist ITGWU could hardly have been greater. If the Boilermakers could afford the luxury of benefit, the ITGWU emphasised protection. And without an apprenticeship system to maintain a scarcity of labour, protection had to mean militancy. Larkin's union was largely made up of dockers to begin with, and remained a force of unskilled labourers in the main. Its early, revolutionary years took it on a roller-coaster ride. The 1913 lockout may have been heroic, but it left the ITGWU battered and bankrupt. Drained by the defeat and the burden of running an organisation in retreat, Larkin handed the union over to James Connolly and headed to America in search of a new career in 1914. The ITGWU suffered further disruption after Connolly took the Citizen Army into the Easter Rising. Liberty Hall was shelled, members were interned, and Connolly was executed by the British on 12 May 1916. The tide turned in 1917, as the impact of the First World War on the Irish economy extended from production in the shipyards and engineering plants to consumption of food. Labour's bargaining position was strengthened by the introduction of compulsory tillage orders to ease the food supply crisis. The number of farm labourers was in steady decline, but they still made up almost 200,000 out of 900,000 waged workers in Ireland. Waterford was one of four counties in Ireland that had more than two labourers to each farmer. The tillage orders in turn created the first labour shortage in agriculture since the Napoleonic wars, compelling the introduction of an Agricultural Wages Board in September 1917 to set minimum rates of pay in order to keep workers on the land. Wage movements on the land had begun in the spring of 1917. Initially, labourers revitalised local land and labour associations and demanded land redistribution and more plots of land. By 1918, local associations were being absorbed into the ITGWU and focusing on wages. In 1916 the ITGWU had 5,000 members. By 1920 it had 120,000, 60,000 of them in agriculture.[9] Organisers like Baird would have their work cut out attempting to 'hold the harvest' in the slump that followed the wartime economic boom.

'Rotten Prods', the derogatory Unionist term for their Ulster Protestant opponents and widely applied in 1920, are beginning to receive some attention. One could argue, as Morrissey does, for the existence of a dissident, democratic and republican tradition among non-conformists since the United Irishmen of the 1790s and for a predisposition of Presbyterians to support the Liberal Party, as was the case in Britain.[10] In Ulster, the tendency was modified by the perception of the Liberals as soft on Irish nationalism. Yet many northern Presbyterians did incline to the Liberals. As late as the 1880s, Catholics and Presbyterians in Derry allied against the Tories, who controlled the Corporation and were identified with the Church of Ireland.[11] Wrangles over parading strained relations and William Gladstone's conversion to Home Rule dealt a body blow to Ulster Liberalism, though the tradition remained of some significance politically up to the third Home Rule crisis.

It is harder to defend the notion of a specifically Protestant custom of dissent within the Labour movement. Parr and Edwards' celebratory articles on the 'rotten Prod tradition' amount to little more than a list of radical or socialist Protestants.[12] It would have been remarkable if there had been none. The wonder is that there were not more. Greer and Walker write of a more moderate type of dissident in biographical reviews of four 'awkward Prods', and argue persuasively that their ethnic identity and religious values influenced their politics.[13] That may be, but they were mavericks rather than outcrops of a tendency with the ideological coherence and sizable grassroots base of Ulster Liberalism. Historically, trade unionists had as much reason as Presbyterians to lean to the Liberals. Labour organisation in Ulster was largely an extension of the cross-channel Labour movement, and in Britain, the Liberals were the party of labour up to the 1900s and embraced a caucus of Liberal-Labourites. Moreover, the Unionists were allied to the Tories and anti-Labour. Even so, after the first Home Rule crisis in 1886, Belfast trades council distanced itself from the Lib-Labs, and declined to accept the syllogism that Home Rule was a democratic demand, Labour men were democrats, and therefore trade unionists should accept Home Rule. The idea of a dichotomy between Labour and nationalism made it easier for Labourites to avoid the constitutional question, and the perception of nationalist Ireland as priest-ridden provided an excuse for opposing Home Rule. Belfast's most famous Labour leader in the early twentieth century, William Walker, would be strongly pro-Union. Nonetheless, there was a difference between being pro-Union and pro-Unionist. Walker always opposed the Unionist Party for its Toryism. For all his protestations of opposition to Home Rule, he was the original 'rotten Prod' in that it was he who began, in 1903, a form of Labour politics that Unionists found unacceptable in normal times and intolerable in moments of crisis. There was nothing peculiarly Protestant about that politics. It was conventional Labourism, embraced by workers from both communities, and the subsequent expulsions, in 1912 and 1920, differed from previous expulsions in victimising both Catholics and Protestants. While the former were targeted for their religion and the latter for their politics, it was not in the politics but in the victimisation that the Protestants were singled out.

Baird was not unusual as a 'rotten Prod'. He was one of hundreds of union activists who veered away from the amalgamateds to Irish Labour in consequence of the 44 hours engineering strike in 1919, victimisation in Belfast's workplace expulsions in 1920, and the willingness of British unions to accept wage cuts with the onset of the slump. But he was exceptional in leaving a written record, however truncated, of his opinions and values, in going on to make the journey from shipyard to farmyard, and in finding himself running foul of the Free State Labour movement too. His is a rare story, not just of a man too radical for Belfast but of one of the subalterns of the failed and forgotten social revolution of 1917–23.

CHAPTER I

In the Black Squad

He was a man named Baird, an iron worker by trade.
Senator Patrick Kenny, Seanad Éireann, 1925.[1]

James Baird was born in the townland of Kilclay, near the village of Augher, in the civil parish of Clogher, south Tyrone, on 6 July 1871. His parents were George Baird and his wife Margaret, née Wright. George was born in 1841, and Margaret in 1850. They married on 18 August 1870. George farmed in Kilclay, with a holding of 10 acres about 5 km from the boundary with Monaghan. He registered James's birth in Clogher on 14 July, and signed the certificate with an X. James had just one full brother, John, born in 1873. Their father died that year and Margaret remarried in 1874. Her second husband was also a farmer, of 24 acres, and she bore eight more children. Protestants formed a large minority in Clogher. It is likely that George was Presbyterian, with James being raised in that faith.[2] We can only speculate on James's education from his extant letters, which were composed in a simple, direct style, with legible handwriting, in a careful upright construction, usually immaculate spelling, and a more casual attitude to punctuation.

James said little on his early life other than that his father was a tenant farmer and that he himself was 'a pronounced Home Ruler and socialist since 1893...in the Queen's Island, Belfast...'.[3] Queen's Island was the site of the Harland and Wolff shipyard. If James was a country boy moving to Belfast for the work, he was not alone. Over the nineteenth century the city was transformed from a linen town of some 20,000 people into a major centre of manufacture with, in 1911, a population of almost 387,000. This was all the more remarkable given the steady decline of the 'south and west' – as the southern provinces were called. While both Belfast and Dublin enjoyed a sizable trade in food, drink, and tobacco, Belfast nearly monopolised other sectors of manufacture in Ireland. In 1907, the Belfast region accounted for £19.1 million of Ireland's £20.9 million worth of manufactured exports, excluding food and drink. Economic development entailed a high degree of specialisation in the British market, chiefly in textiles and clothing and shipbuilding and engineering; and the locomotive of growth was the phenomenal expansion of iron and steel shipbuilding from the 1860s in Belfast's two yards, Harland and Wolff, the 'big yard', and Workman, Clark, the 'wee yard'. For their bounty, and the irony, they were also known to Belfast workers as 'the vineyard'.[4] The yards were employing 12,000 by 1890, and 20,000 by 1914. Harland and Wolff recorded 10,504 workers in 1915 and was estimated to have a peak of 26,000 employees in 1919. Shipbuilding in turn relied heavily on Britain's status as a maritime superpower with a global empire, flagging 40 per cent of the world's ships and carrying half its oceanic cargo. The ties binding Belfast with imperial welfare found their most potent symbolism in building Britannia's mighty merchantmen, ocean liners, and warships.

WORK

Like any huge enterprise of its day, Harland and Wolff had a diverse labour force structured in a hierarchy of dozens of grades ranging from 'the hats' – managers, accountants, clerks, typists, timekeepers, and inspectors, so called for their bowler hats – to labourers and a variety of ancillary occupations like caterers, waitresses, charladies, security guards, porters, and messengers. At times there was a fire brigade with an appliance and uniformed firefighters, and bus drivers for the yard's internal transport service. It was a highly status-conscious environment, and where possible a grade would be signalled by clothes such as a hat, a tie, or a jacket. Artisans were the key men, and a shipyard workforce required a high proportion of them – over 40 per cent of employees in Harland and Wolff were skilled manual – with qualifications for as many as 90 trades. Principal among the trades were draughtsmen, platers, caulkers, anglesmiths, rivetters, fitters, electricians, blacksmiths, drillers, plumbers, shipwrights, joiners, and painters. Definitions and demarcation practices were a source of chronic dispute and varied from district to district. 'Joiner', for example, might include carpenter, cabinetmaker, joiner's machinist, and patternmaker. Similarly, boilermakers were no longer just boilersmiths. With the emergence of iron shipbuilding, the term was applied to men making or maintaining a range of steel, iron, or copper vessels for ships. The final and most sophisticated phase of Belfast's industrial revolution, the development of marine engineering in the 1880s and 1890s as the yards 'added value' by opening their own engine shops, created a strong demand for boilermakers.

Baird gave his occupation as 'iron caulker' in the 1901 census. Caulkers made hulls and decks waterproof and upgraded older hulls. The 1893 Royal Commission on Labour defined iron caulkers as:

> Skilled labourers in the shipbuilding, boilermaking, and engineering
> industries who *caulk*, crease, or cut in, the edges, seams, joints, laps, and
> butts, in the combinations of iron plates or bars, after they have left the hands
> of the 'rivetters', in order to make them water-tight, oil-tight, or steam-tight,
> by compressing the material solidly together along the line of contact. In
> some cases red lead is used to fill in the seams, but usually a tool is placed
> against the edge and struck by a hammer, thus turning the edges close in
> against one another.[5]

With platers, anglesmiths, and rivetters they were known as 'the black
squad', a term which took on a peculiar meaning in 'the black north'. It's
probable that James served his time on Queen's Island between 1893 and
1898. The union's registry books record him as worthy brother no.23971,
admitted to the Ballymacarrett no.1 branch on 15 March 1898. He was
relatively old for a man just out of his time and gave his age as 22.[6]

Critical to the wages and status of artisans was the apprenticeship
system. It was vital to maintaining a scarcity of labour, and craftsmen were
notorious for using the apprenticeship fee – higher if the boy's father was
not in the trade – to keep jobs within the family, but the rapid advance of
Belfast shipbuilding in the late nineteenth century created opportunities
for outsiders. Normally an apprenticeship at Harland and Wolff started at
16, though because of the demand for places it was not unusual for lads to
start at 17 or 18, and lasted five years. The boy's parents had to guarantee
his good behaviour, underwritten with a deposit of £2 to £5, and buy his
tool kit, which might be worth up to £6.[7] A caulker's tools might include
two or three types of mallets, a set of caulking chisels, and an array of hooks
or scrapers to clean the seams between the hull or deck planks prior to
caulking. An apprentice was also expected to attend day or evening classes
run by the Board of Education. Those with primary schooling only, would
begin with classes in English, arithmetic, and drawing in their first year.
Subsequent years would involve more applied instruction devised by the
City and Guilds of London. In 1912 an apprentice caulker earned 8s. per
week in his first year, rising incrementally to 12s. per week in his fifth year,
with extra for overtime and less for time lost, for whatever reason, and
fines for infringement of rules. As the black squad were frequently paid 'on
piece', an apprentice caulker might earn 24s. weekly in his third and 30s.
weekly in his final year. As a journeyman, he could earn 33s. per week or,
if paid 'on piece' in a good year when trade was brisk, an average of £3 per
week. By contrast, the 'leading rate' for labourers was 18s.6d. per week.[8]
Yardmen had a reputation for swinging the lead, but being on piece-work
the black squads were known for hard grafting.

Apprenticeships, wage rates, and the organisation of work made
trenchant distinctions between the skilled and the unskilled men who

frequently worked as their assistants. Working practices gave both sides a sense of being competitors in a zero-sum game. Up to the 1890s, boilermakers paid their assistants, known as plater's helpers, directly. When the helpers were organised by National Amalgamated Union of Labour (NAUL), they struck to end the practice. The helpers in Belfast were relatively quick to unionise. The NAUL had been founded in February 1889 as the United Tyne and District Labourers' Association, in response to the exclusion of labourers from existing unions. It began organising in Belfast in 1890 as the Tyneside and National Labour Union. It became the NAUL in 1892, and Belfast was one of its strongholds. Within six years it had 2,000 members in nine branches in the city.[9] The Royal Commission on Labour went so far as to say: 'its chief antagonists have been, not the employers, but the skilled organisations with which its members come into contact. Its most serious contentions have been with the Boilermakers' and Shipbuilders' Society...'.[10] Other crafts too were a threat. Of the 40 strikes in Belfast engineering and shipbuilding between 1888 and 1913, 14 were demarcation disputes.[11] Bob Getgood, an official for textile workers in the Amalgamated Transport and General Workers' Union in the mid twentieth century, was acerbic about the shipyard craftsmen and the power they had over the labourers.

> And there was craft pride – I must give him credit for his craft pride. But he hadn't the broad human touch of the other fellow who carried the mud for him... There was no association. The labourers herded together, went off together. But an odd one would have curried favour with a foreman but [was] much more likely to be currying favour with his skilled employee or his fellow employee. He was anxious to be on good terms with him because his job was more secure. He felt that if he could be on good terms with the craftsmen then his value to the craftsmen was seen and if a choice had to be made, he was likely to be retained in preference to the fellow who was probably a better man but harder to work with.[12]

The chief drawback of the job was the nagging insecurity that went with the irregularity of work in consequence of the weather or a dearth of orders for new vessels. 'Perhaps no industry in Great Britain is [as] subject to such fluctuations', observed the Boilermakers' secretary to the Royal Commission on Labour.[13] Between 1902 and 1920 unemployment averaged 6 per cent among trade unionists in the Belfast shipyards, in 18 quarters it exceeded 10 per cent, and in the depressions of 1903–5 and 1908–9 it was over 20 per cent.[14] And then there were the health risks. The shipyards had acquired a public notoriety as hazardous places. James Connolly thought compensation for accidents should be a major item on the unions' agenda, and blamed the long working day and piecework or 'rushing', for creating systems 'red with the blood of the workers':

It has been computed that some seventeen lives were lost on the *Titanic* before she left the Lagan; a list of the maimed and hurt and of those suffering from minor injuries, as a result of the accidents at any one of those big ships would read like a roster of the wounded after a battle upon the Indian frontier. The public reads and passes on, but fails to comprehend the totality of suffering involved. But it all means lives ruined, fair prospects blighted, homes devastated, crippled wrecks of manhood upon the streets, or widows and orphans to eat the bread of poverty and pauperism.

Add to this an army of insurance doctors paid, to belittle the injury, and declare the injured to be well and hearty, a host of lawyers whose practice depends upon their success in confusing honest workers when endeavouring, amid unfamiliar surroundings, to tell the truth about the mangling or killing of their workmates, and, finally, a hostile judge treating every applicant for just compensation as if they were known and habitual criminals, and you have a faint idea of one side of industrial life (and death) in the North of Ireland.[15]

The industry was subject to the Factory Acts, of course, but inspections were rare. Greater concern arose from the Employers' Liability Act. The rising cost of insurance premiums led to a push for tougher safety measures and a parliamentary enquiry. The more serious injuries arose from falls or being hit by falling articles. There were 1,510 falls in shipyards by the Lagan, Clyde, and Tyne in 1912, 62 of them fatal, and 1,415 injuries sustained from falling objects, 15 of them fatal. Boilermakers commonly went deaf at an early age, and caulkers would 'tune' their mallets by extending the slots or drilling holes in them to make the 'pinging' less sharp and found ways of synchronising the sound of multiple mallets to make it less grating on the ear. Caulking also entailed injury to the eyes unless goggles were worn, which they usually were not as they hindered vision. Half the bonuses for accidents paid by the Boilermakers' Society in 1920 involved optical damage. The ASE found that the two greatest complaints of Belfast men related to glasses and poor sanitation. Engineers commonly suffered from deteriorating eyesight in their 40s, but dared not wear spectacles for fear of being let go. The unhealthiness of the job was made worse by poor sanitation, restricted washing facilities, and the proximity of primitive toilet and canteen areas.[16]

LIFE

Living conditions in Belfast were by no means easy. Labourers' wages were below the UK average outside the shipyards, unskilled men suffered chronic underemployment, and public health was poor, the city having been built on a swamp.[17] But for skilled men in the metal trades, Belfast had its advantages. Skilled rates were above the UK average, food prices were relatively low, and housing was good and relatively cheap. As the last of the great cities of the British industrial revolution, Belfast had plenty of purpose-built working-class accommodation in its signature 'Coronation streets'. In 1901, 90 per cent of the city's population lived in dwellings of four rooms or more, compared with 26 per cent in Glasgow. Three rooms in Belfast could be rented for between 2s.6d. and 5s. per week, compared with around 7s. in Glasgow.[18] Even Connolly was impressed: 'Belfast is a distinct improvement upon Dublin. Municipally, it can compare favourably with any similar city in Great Britain...The homes of the poor are better, house rent is lower, and the city is cleaner and healthier than Dublin.'[19]

On 10 December 1898 James married Frances Lavina Miller, also cited as Frances Lavinia, in Saint Matthew's Church of Ireland, Lurganure Road, Broomhedge, near Lisburn. It was the convention in Protestant inter-denominational marriages for the wedding to take place in the bride's church and for the wife to take her husband's religion. Presbyterians in Ulster commonly regarded themselves as socially superior to Anglicans, and not all Church of Ireland parishes welcomed mixed marriages. Frances was living at the time in Broughmore. Again James falsified his age, giving it as 25, which made him two years younger than his birth cert. While it was not unusual for working class people of the time to be unsure of their age – James gave his age in the 1901 census as 28 – his correct age was given on his death certificate. Frances was 18 and one of 12 children of Jane Miller, née Behan in 1847. Frances was born in Tipperary in 1880, and was cited on the marriage certificate simply as 'spinster'. Her father, Robert, was a former Head Constable in the Royal Irish Constabulary (RIC), Head Constable being the highest rank below officer level.[20] Born in 1835, he had married Jane in 1865. The Bairds settled first in Ribble Street, east Belfast, a terraced street of two-up, two-down houses off the Newtownards Road. In 1901, the census listed James, Frances, and Nora Baird as resident in Ardenvohr Street, another terrace of two-up, two-downs, with an overwhelmingly Protestant occupancy, in Belfast's Ormeau district. All three were recorded as Presbyterians, though Nora would be known in Australia as 'staunchly Anglican'. In 1907, Nora recalled, they were living in Holywood, half-way to Bangor. Frances was not working outside the home, but a salient memory of Nora's was minding the younger children when her parents were 'out on business' and escorting them to school. The Bairds would have six children: after Nora in 1900, Geneve was born in 1902, Eileen in 1905, Kathleen in 1908, George in 1910, and Helene in 1917.[21] They were a close and loving family.

The Irish names given to three of the daughters may be a clue to their parents' outlook. In Australia, Nora would be nicknamed 'Ireland'.[22] Her father's views on religion can only be conjectured. In 1905 he proposed to Belfast trades council that it deplore efforts to foster alliances between the non-conformist Free Church and the labour movement in Britain. It says something for the influence of non-conformism on the council that the motion was passed so narrowly, by 15-13 votes.[23] At the same time, like William Walker, he was a brother of the Independent Order of Rechabites, a temperance and benefit society founded in Salford in 1835; his branch, or tent, being the Westbourne in east Belfast. Founded in 1887, the Westbourne was one of some 40 tents in the city, and one of the biggest with 270 members in 1899. In Britain, the Order stood 'solidly for equality, fraternity, justice' and women's rights and was associated with the Liberal Party. Of the 26 Rechabites elected to parliament in 1906, 23 were Liberals and two (Arthur Henderson and David Shackleton) were Labourites. The 26th was Tom Sloan, a semi-skilled worker in Harland and Wolff who had founded the Independent Orange Order as a populist alternative to its conservative namesake and was a leading member of the Belfast Protestant Association.[24] Sloan's victory in the Belfast South by-election in 1902 was partly financed by the non-conformist chairman of Harland and Wolff, William Pirrie. The Rechabites in Belfast had a strong connection with the shipyards and Presbyterianism, and the Order was the biggest friendly society in Ulster.[25] In another illustration of the Order's radical reputation, and one the mature Baird would surely have approved of, the London Connolly Club held 'successful dances' in the capital's Rechabites Hall in 1939.[26]

THE UNION

Baird's trade union was typical of the 'new model unions' formed by Britain's 'labour aristocrats'. When Baird joined it was open only to the five classes of mechanics in iron and steel shipbuilding: angle-iron smiths, platers, rivetters, caulkers, and holders-up. Labourers were 'altogether excluded', and a brother proposing for admission 'any person with whom he is not perfectly acquainted' was liable to a fine of 30s. Subscription rates were high at 1s.3d. per week. There were three grades of membership: the first class were those who had served an apprenticeship to the trade, second class members were those who had worked in the industry for five years, and third class was open to others of the five classes of mechanics. The third class paid a lower subscription and received no benefits except strike pay. The craft unions were paragons of subsidiarity – allowing the maximum autonomy to branches – and prudent governance. The Boilermakers' executive council even claimed to be impartial in disputes:

> For it represents the union as a whole, and not any of the individual districts that successive disputes may affect. It does not conduct the meetings of the

men concerned in a dispute, but simply deals with any business that may be sent to its office. Recognising the ultimate community of interest between labour and capital, the council is guided in its actions by the interest of the trade as a whole. It does not hold a brief for one side. Its independent character has enabled it to be a specially beneficial means of controlling disputes.[27]

An average of 95 per cent of its income annually was disbursed on sick, accident, out-of-work, superannuation, and charitable benefits. Even by the standards of the craft unions, its expenditure on disputes was low. In 1893 the Boilermakers' district agent for the North of Ireland reported a membership of 1,800 and no non-unionists in Belfast. Their relations with the employers were 'good'.[28]

The Boilermakers were also part of the Federation of Engineering and Shipbuilding Trades (FEST), one of a number of confederations in Belfast and by far the most powerful. The FEST had been founded in 1891, in response to the creation of an employers' alliance and to arbitrate in demarcation disputes. Its Belfast district committee dated from 20 June 1898. In 1920 it represented 60,000 workers, compared with the trades council's 15,000 or so.[29] The roll call of affiliates illustrated its reach and the complexity of Belfast trade unionism: the Associated Blacksmiths; the Boilermakers; the Brassfounders' and United Coppersmiths' Association; the National Society of Coppersmiths; the Braziers and Metal Workers; the Electrical Trades Union; the National Amalgamated Furnishing Trades Association; the Friendly Society of Ironfounders; the Iron Steel and Metal Dressers; the NAUL; the United Machine Workers; the National Amalgamated Painters and Decorators; the United Patternmakers' Association; the United Operative Plumbers; the Association of Ship Constructors and Shipwrights; the Amalgamated Society of Smiths and Strikers; the Sheetmetal Workers and Braziers; the Steam Engine Makers; the Woodcutting Machinists; the Amalgamated Union of Upholsterers; and the Amalgamated Cabinetmakers, Carpenters, and Joiners (ASCJ).[30] A notable omission from the list was the ASE. It had affiliated between 1905 and 1914 only to withdraw after failing to persuade other unions to join it in the creation of an industrial union during the merger-mania that affected British Labour after 1912.

The confederations functioned, among other things, as an alternative to Belfast trades council, and partially explain its under-achievement. Arguably, there were two Labour movements in the city; one focused on the trades council, whose supporters tended to be small, weak local unions in textiles and construction, with affiliations to the Irish Trades Union Congress (ITUC); and the other based in the shipyards and the metal trades and made up of British-based unions with a stronger bargaining power, Conservative in politics and wary of the trades council and the ITUC as too sympathetic to Irish nationalism.[31] The Belfast Boilermakers, for example, did not engage with the ITUC and were represented minimally and intermittently on Belfast trades council, despite the council's repeated efforts to attract them. At one meeting they were singled out for 'not taking an interest' and it was agreed to send them a deputation.[32] Baird became active on the council in late 1903 and contested the elections for vice-president in January 1906, winning 11 votes, 21 less than the victor, Joseph Harris. Baird served on the council's committee of auditors and pursued various initiatives to raise revenue and curb expenditure, including the end of honorariums for council officers. His preoccupations at council meetings were largely with his union, demarcation lines, and the shipyardmen. He said nothing on the race-related questions debated at council meetings, such as the Boer War, imperialism, or Chinese labour.[33] One exception to the parochialism arose from his involvement with the Right to Work Committee, which had branches throughout the UK and aimed to educate public opinion to pressure parliament. Baird proposed that the trades council organise an unemployed demonstration, with bands and banners. Now it was the council's turn to be parsimonious, and the idea was rejected as too expensive. Baird and Thomas Johnston, secretary of the recently established Belfast Socialist Society, went ahead with a lobby to Belfast Corporation in January 1906, suggesting the council might create work through land reclamation and reafforestation programmes. The Lord Mayor, Sir Daniel Dixon, replied that these were political questions and the Corporation 'never interfered with politics'. It was not for nothing that Walker dubbed him 'Dodger Dan'. After the unconscious humour Dixon ventured a joke worthy of Marie Antoinette, quipping 'You all look pretty well anyhow'. The city fathers sniggered. Baird and Johnston made their excuses and left. Baird resigned as trades council auditor in February 1906 to make way for an ASE nominee, and by the end of the year he had ceased to attend council meetings.[34] He retained an interest in politics and sought a nomination as a Boilermakers' delegate to the British Labour Party on at least one occasion.

POLITICAL FORMATION

A clue as to why Baird became a socialist and a Home Ruler is found in an article he wrote for the *Voice of Labour* in 1919, 'A townsman's views on land ownership'.[35] Demanding 'the land for the people', he argued 'our people' must 'own the land and live as freemen or remain slaves for he who owns the land owns the people'. On the face of it, land ownership was an odd topic for a Belfast yardman. Neither would being the son of a tenant farmer have predisposed him to the taxation or nationalisation of land. Extending his ideas on public control of industry and education to land, the article suggested that Baird had been influenced by Henry George's *Progress and Poverty: An Inquiry into the Cause of Industrial Depressions and of Increase of Want with Increase of Wealth: The Remedy* (1879), a seminal work for many in Britain on the road to socialism. George had had a Belfast champion in the Revd John Bruce Wallace, a Congregational Church minister at Cliftonpark Avenue. In 1884, Bruce Wallace helped to establish the Irish Land Restoration Society in Belfast, and drew support from a scattering of Land Leaguers, Home Rulers, Liberals, and trade unionists. Robert McClung recalled one of its meetings in the Ulster Hall entering Belfast Labour folklore for sparking an acrimonious exchange between Wallace and Revd 'Roaring' Hugh Hanna. From 1889, Wallace was prominent in the Belfast Radical Association, which ran a reading room on Royal Avenue. As a socialist – of the Christian anarchist variety – he was particularly keen to evangelise among workers, and to that end founded the *Belfast Evening Star*. It concentrated on news of the Radical Association and issues like land nationalisation, unemployment, housing, sanitation, municipal reform, and the eight hour day. And it was pitched primarily at Protestant workers, to win them to Home Rule. Wallace believed that socialists should accept the democratic and radical case for Home Rule and that Protestant workers could be converted through socialism. When the *Evening Star* folded, Wallace replaced it with the *Belfast Weekly Star*, which proposed to devote 'a considerable amount of space' to the trades.[36]

Wallace addressed at least three meetings on Queen's Island in 1890. One of his published appeals targeted the yardmen specifically. 'Let for instance a thousand intelligent and sober young men belonging to the ship building trades, receiving perhaps 30s a week, delay marrying for a couple of years and lay by 10s per week. They could then build a co-operative ship building company with a capital of £50,000'.[37] At his third meeting on the Island Wallace was attacked by 'a gang of lads' for his views on the Orange Order and had to be rescued by their seniors. George's concern to avoid the boom-slump cycle would have an obvious appeal for the chronically insecure shipyardmen. In the aftermath of the world war, Baird predicted that globalisation would undermine the privileged position of European workers:

> The artificial conditions which at present prevail cannot endure much longer, and our capitalists will, as a matter of business, employ the labour which is cheap, without regard to colour or race; the cotton mills of India and Japan will be pitted against Lancashire; the industrious Chinaman will be taught to build ships; British steamers will be manned by Lascars; while the men who

manned the Navy and Mercantile Marine during the war will be cast aside unless they are prepared to offer themselves upon the altar of cheapness.[38]

Taxation of land and public 'possession of the soil' could provide the resources for a new and less vulnerable industrial base, though he did not specify how. Baird's belief that 'every article of food or clothing comes from the land', also reflected a mind shaped by linenopolis, and its roots in flax-growing. The topic evidently reflected mature consideration. When a motion for the taxation of land values came before Belfast trades council in 1906, and Baird moved an amendment in favour of land nationalisation.[39]

The great political anomaly for the shipyard unions was that they were part of the British Labour movement, and the formation in 1900 of the Labour Representation Committee (LRC), later the British Labour Party, by the Social Democratic Federation, the Independent Labour Party (ILP), co-operators, and trade unionists indicated that cross-channel unions were moving left. Nationally, the Boilermakers voted 26,478 to 8,905 to affiliate to the LRC. Members paid a political levy of 3d per week. In May 1903 Baird was a Boilermakers' delegate in Ye Olde Castle Restaurant, Castle Place, to initiate British Labour politics in Belfast. It was a fatal development, that would set Labour on a collision course with Unionists. The key problem for Belfast Labour was not the religious divide, but the contradiction between the Tory politics of the bulk of Protestant workers and the Liberalism or Labourism of its British role models. When the council entered municipal politics in 1896, it tried to maintain its own local party, which allowed it to enjoy good relations with the Unionist grandees who controlled the Old Town Hall, but proved an expensive and fractious enterprise. Walker and others more critical of the Conservatives waited in the long grass. The *Belfast Evening Telegraph*'s labour correspondent derided them as a stage army who still managed to 'run' the trades council.

> It would be quite possible for a dozen or so persons, with a good deal of time on their hands to form, say the I.L.P – Indigent Literary Party – Belfast Branch, between 3 and 5 on every Saturday; be Trades Council delegates from 5 to 7.30; disguised in an unaccustomed smile to pose as Bugle Blowing Brotherhooders from 7.30 to 8 o'clock; and finish up the evening as the Griskin Elevationing League.[40]

Moreover, the *Telegraph*'s labour correspondent, Edward McInnes, was a Labour councillor, a declared Conservative, i.e., Unionist, and an official of the NAUL.[41] Based mainly on semi-skilled men in the shipyards, the NAUL was an important centre of anti-socialism in the Belfast Labour movement.

The LRC promised a more substantial party, independent of the Liberals and less identified with Irish nationalism. With the Tories in power and Home Rule off the agenda, circumstances were looking propitious, and Walker persuaded the trades council to create a Belfast section of the LRC. For Walker, unity in the British Labour movement was the answer to Ireland's problems. The Olde Castle Restaurant gathering inaugurated a brief purple patch for the Belfast left. The star speakers were Keir Hardie, MP, admired as Labour's founding-father, and James Ramsay MacDonald, who would become Britain's first Labour prime minister. Delegates attended from the Co-operative Society, the Clarion Fellowship, the Belfast Ethical Society, the Ruskin Hall Education League, the ILP, and 32 trade unions. Even McInnes extended a grudging congratulations, describing the occasion as 'splendid' and 'most representative'.[42] Baird was active, but not prominent, in Labour politics. He was scarcely mentioned, for example, in the *Belfast Labour Chronicle*, organ of the trades council and LRC between 1904 and 1906, nor did he hold officer posts in the LRC.

There are hints of tension between Baird and Walker. As auditor, Baird tried to make the *Belfast Labour Chronicle* more accountable to the council. Run by Walker's aides, one could be forgiven for thinking the *Chronicle*'s primary purpose was to get Walker to Westminster, and Walker did not take kindly to criticism. His trademark high, white collar gave his appearance a certain hauteur that was not entirely deceptive. There was a perfunctoriness to the *Chronicle*'s coverage of the Right to Work lobby to the Corporation. Following the 1906 general election Baird wrote to the paper complaining that it faulted the LRC for contesting Croydon, splitting the vote, and facilitating a Tory victory. The *Chronicle*, he wrote, should champion Labour alone.[43] But Baird would appear to have sided with Walker on the latter's hugely controversial endorsement of the Belfast Protestant Association's programme in the 1905 by-election in Belfast North. In a war to the knife with 'Dodger Dan' Dixon, the endorsement was a desperate ploy to win the votes of Sloan's Independent Orangemen. For many trade unionists, in Belfast and beyond, collaboration with the ultra-sectarian Protestant Association was beyond the Pale and it blackened Walker's reputation forever. There was a forgotten echo of the battle. In January 1906 William Davison, a Sloanite and a municipal candidate in St George's ward, sought trade council backing, promising to 'stand up on all occasions with Mr Walker and Mr [Alex] Boyd [Independent Orangeman and secretary of the Municipal Employés Association] on behalf of the democracy'.[44] When it was proposed that no action be taken, Baird moved an amendment that the council offer its 'moral support' as Davison favoured the labour cause and 'he might go as straight as some of their labour representatives in the past'. The amendment was carried 23-13. After Baird was kicked out of

Harland and Wolff in 1920, Boyd defended the expulsions.[45] Walker was
unrepentant about chasing Sloan. Even after he failed to win Belfast North
a second time in the 1906 general election, he was keen to exploit every
opportunity. When Baird moved his amendment for land nationalisation
on Belfast trades council in May 1906, Walker, as chairman, ruled it out
of order and then proposed the council ask Sloan and Joe Devlin, recently
elected MPs for Belfast South and West, to get Ireland included in the
government measure for taxing land values in 1907. Devlin's inclusion was
political cover. The motion was carried.[46]

Baird made a more public intervention in the 1907 Westminster by-
election, when Walker made his third and final bid for Belfast North in a
straight fight with George 'Orange' Clark, a partner in Workman, Clark.
Again the Unionists traduced the 'Radical-Socialist-Home Rule-anything
you like candidate', as the *Belfast Evening Telegraph* dubbed Walker.[47] Walker
pleaded that there was no better way of strengthening the Union than
joining a British party. But for Unionists, Labour was a Home Rule party,
and for boilermakers, the unexpected arrival of John Hill, Glasgow-based
organising delegate of their union, to speak for Walker caused 'ructions'.
The press made some mileage out of boilermen in hot water. A dinner-
hour meeting of boilermakers in the north yard of Harland's repudiated
Hill. As chairman, Baird convened the union's Belfast district committee
to condemn the action in the north yard.[48] Hill's presence in Belfast was
not disinterested. He had been suggested as a candidate for Belfast North
by Ramsay MacDonald should Walker not stand. In September 1907
he defeated Walker to win the nomination for a by-election in Liverpool
Kirkdale. As an ILP'er, he ran on a radical programme, and although a
committed Congregationalist, Kirkdale Conservatives slandered him as
pro-Catholic, irreligious, and anti-family, to such an extent that the Labour
Party described it as 'the most disagreeable' campaign it had ever fought.
The outcome too was disagreeable, as the Tory majority was increased.[49]

Curiously, the Bairds were not returned in the 1911 census for
Ireland or Britain with the exception of Eileen, who was living with her
grandparents Robert and Jane Miller in Broughmore, where Robert had a
farm to supplement his pension from the RUC. James was then secretary
of the Ballymacarrett no. 1 branch of the boilermakers, and exercised about
reforms of the society's complex system of dues payments and benefits.[50] The
union had eight branches in the city in Baird's time, four covering 'Belfast'
and four for Ballymacarrett in east Belfast, where skilled yardmen tended
to live, in sight of the cranes of Harland and Wolff. The no. 1 branch had
about 330 first class members in 1920, 30 or so in each of the other grades,
and met in the aptly named Vulcan Hall, Dee Street, off the Newtownards
Road.[51] Apart from his signature on branch notices in the press, Baird did

not come to public notice in Belfast before 1918 and in 1920 the *Belfast News-Letter* thought him a Scotsman.[52] In 1918 James was living in 372 Beersbridge Road, east Belfast, and still secretary of the Ballymacarrett no.1 branch.[53] A sixth and final child, Helene Jane Emily Matilda, had arrived on 1 December 1917 and by 1919 the family had ascended the housing ladder again, to 43 Willowholme Street, a comfortable mid-terrace red-brick villa with four spacious bedrooms and small gardens front and back, in east Belfast.[54] Space was probably a consideration too for the eldest girl, Nora, who was now making her way in the Royal Academy of Music to a career in piano teaching, and would give lessons from her home. Helene remembered singing as a constant feature of family life and she would become Nora's most brilliant pupil.

During the war, it was said, money grew on the tops of the bushes. So too did prices, food shortages, and class consciousness. Shopfloor unrest, and the shop stewards' movement on Clydeside in particular, gave the Boilermakers a reputation for militancy. The Bolshevik revolution led to a strong communist presence in the union, exemplified by Harry Pollitt, who would become secretary general of the Communist Party of Great Britain.[55] In Ulster, by contrast, in his work and in his union, Baird was operating in a very caste-conscious and aggressively Protestant environment, where the black squad did not define themselves purely by their trade. Toasting the King or singing the national anthem was usual at the social concerts and smokers of the Ballymacarrett no.1 branch. The swaggering style was captured by John Hanna, a nominee of the Ulster Unionist Council. Horace Plunkett noted his tasteless but effective contribution to the Irish Convention, the British government's post-Rising effort at a constitutional settlement, or a constitutional settlement acceptable to the British government.

> He belonged to what was known as the 'Black Squad', the highest paid workmen in the British Isles, many of whom 'had money in the Three per Cents' [war bonds], some, himself included, being the proud possessors of the last luxury of the idle rich, a motor car. He told us that the organised industrial workers of Ireland were too closely affiliated to the great trade unions across the channel to look with favour upon any weakening of the political link.[56]

In fact, Hanna was a shipwright, and worked in wood. At the same time, the shipyards were hotbeds of militancy in the later war years and immediately after. Belfast's wider Labour politics was enjoying a resurgence, moving left and moving closer to Dublin. The interface between these two worlds was becoming increasingly edgy, and Baird was drawn to the vortex.

A CONTRARY POLITICS

Shipyardmen prided themselves as the shock-troops of loyalism, and had been prominent in sectarian riots in 1857, and in attempts to expel Catholic workers from the yards in 1864, 1886, 1893, and 1901.[57] Catholics formed 28 per cent of shipyardmen in 1861 and 11 per cent in 1911, when police estimated that some 6,000 shipyard workers were in Unionist clubs and Orange lodges in their workplaces.[58] On 14 April 1916 a group of young Islandmen rammed a lorry into an anti-conscription meeting organised by the ITUC at the Custom House steps, Belfast's speakers' corner. After the crowd dispersed in panic, rioting followed in the city centre as rival gangs fought late into the night.[59] No unions in the Belfast metal trades were affiliated to the ITUC in 1919. Where these unions had members in Dublin, as did the two biggest shipyard unions, the ASE and the ASCJ, they affiliated their Dublin branches only.[60] For the boilermakers, the affiliation to Congress was not only confined to the Dublin lodge but very intermittent. As late as 1959, a study by two Quaker academics, Barritt and Carter, found that the Boilermakers' Society in Northern Ireland had no Catholic branch secretaries. Its successor union, the General, Municipal, and Boilermakers, was one of the first organisations to be prosecuted – for discrimination against its own Catholic members – under the Fair Employment Act (1976). Many believed it was just the most egregious example of a much bigger malaise within the unions. In the ASE's successor, the Amalgamated Engineering Union (AEU), just 12 per cent of branch secretaries were Catholic.[61] Andrew Boyd, an apprentice machine turner in Harland and Wolff in the 1940s, was advised by his branch secretary to join the freemasons if he wished to 'get on' in the AEU. Boyd reckoned the masons were well placed throughout trade union officialdom in Northern Ireland.[62]

The labour question had been a flickering theme in Unionism since the first Home Rule crisis, when Belfast's anti-Gladstonian Liberals sent Westminster an embassy of trade unionists. 'Labour Unionists' came into common currency during the third Home Rule crisis to describe Unionist clubs that were predominantly working class. For the Ulster Unionist Council, 'labour Unionism' was of use primarily in the propaganda war in Britain, to counter Liberal or Nationalist arguments that Unionism was a movement of landlords and businessmen. Unionist politicians ignored official Labour, and repeatedly spurned overtures from the ITUC. Contacts with Belfast trades council withered once it affiliated to the British Labour Party.[63] No less than 102 delegations of British workingmen, usually from Conservative Associations, visited Ireland in 1914 on 'Home Rule study tours'. On 7 April 1914 the Unionist press carried an appeal to British colleagues, signed 'On behalf of the overwhelming body of trade unionists in Ulster' by 20 men, members mainly of unions in the shipyards.[64] Sectarian solidarity was too valuable politically to permit a similar charm offensive in Ireland. Irish Protestants outside the moral community of loyalism were traitors, and weeding them out of employment was 'a matter of long-standing discussion in Orange and Unionist circles'.[65] In July 1912, some 3,000 workers were expelled from the shipyards and engineering plants; in retaliation, it was claimed, for an assault by Hibernians on a Presbyterian Sunday school outing in Castledawson, County Derry. Unlike previous expulsions, radicals of all religions were targeted, and about 600 of the expelled men were Protestants, victimised for being Labourites, Liberals, or Independent Orangemen. By the end of July over 8,000 were destitute in Belfast in consequence of the assaults and subsequent rioting. D.R. Campbell, a senior official with the ITUC and Belfast trades council, helped to organise an Expelled Workers' Committee, which raised relief funds and lobbied the authorities to protect those willing to go back to work.[66] The ITUC's Parliamentary Committee made similar representations to John Redmond and the British Labour Party.[67] But Campbell could not persuade Belfast trades council to associate itself with the expellees. Instead it suggested that he act discretely. Though Unionist leaders had condemned the violence, the council declined to mention the disturbances in its annual report for 1912, deciding that any reference would stir up controversy.

The trades council's timidity was all the more remarkable as the council had scant influence in the employments directly affected, where the most powerful labour bureaucracy was the Belfast district committee of the FEST. Baird remembered being on a union delegation to RIC city commissioner T. J. Smith on 5 July seeking protection for Catholic workers wanting to draw their pay. Smith, later Sir T. J., told them that police intervention would make things worse. Previous attempts to curb sectarianism had led to a history of animosity between yardmen and the RIC.[68] Only when Harland and Wolff threatened to close the yard did the FEST district committee repudiate the 'lawlessness' and 'terrorism', and its affiliates promise to curb the hot-heads. On 30 July the boilermakers similarly promised to 'do their best' to prevent trouble after management proposed to suspend work'.[69] Normality returned in August 1912. Few of the expellees got their jobs back.

What would be hailed as the symbolic birth of labour Unionism took place at a 'monster demonstration' in the Ulster Hall on 29 April 1914, convened by Thompson Donald and William Grant, both former officers of the Shipwrights' Association, and Joseph Cunningham, sometime secretary of the Belfast district council of the ASE.[70] There were predictable sideswipes at Redmond, the Liberals, and Catholic clerics, but the focal point of criticism was Labour. Interestingly, the speakers ignored the ITUC, saving their scorn for Belfast trades council, and MacDonald and his MPs, growing fat on £400 a year.[71] As the First World War drew to a close the emphasis in labour Unionism shifted from presenting a better image to British Liberals to combatting socialism. Richard Dawson Bates, secretary of the Ulster Unionist Council, argued:

> many of the unions are controlled by officials who hold Home Rule views. The result has been frequently [that] the opinions of the working class in Belfast on the question of the union are misrepresented in England and elsewhere. The absence of such means as I have indicated above frequently leads younger members of the working class to Socialist, i.e. extreme, organisations run by the ILP where they are educated in views very different to those held by our body...[72]

A Trades Unionist Watch Committee met in the Old Town Hall on 26 October 1917 to discuss labour representation on the Ulster Unionist Council, a workingmen's Unionist association was formed within the Council in May 1918, and in June Sir Edward Carson gave the process another push with the foundation of the Ulster Unionist Labour Association (UULA). In the temper of the times, 'Labour' was thought to be more appropriate than 'workingmen's'. The UULA claimed 30,000 members, though its branch structure remained feeble.[73] Initially, it aimed expressly to oppose official Labour, but as workers gave little support to so-called 'Ulster' alternatives to British-based unions – such as the Ulster Workers' Union – the UULA came to accept the British unions industrially, while rejecting their politics. Andrew Boyd recalled the AEU as controlled by the UULA up to the mid-1920s.[74]

Dawson Bates had grounds for concern. While most Labour MPs were sceptical of nationalism, Irish nationalism especially, they saw Home Rule as a simple matter of democracy. Supporting the Unionists was not an option given that they were hand in glove with the Conservatives, and partition would institutionalise sectarianism in Ulster. For similar reasons, most Belfast Labourites regarded Home Rule as unfortunate and undesirable, but preferable to partition. At Easter 1912 four of Belfast's five ILP branches agreed to join with Connolly's Socialist Party of Ireland in a new all-Ireland venture, the Independent Labour Party (of Ireland). What had been Walker's own branch stayed loyal to their hero's abiding conviction that external links should be with the British Labour. Walker himself had forsaken Labour for a job with the government's health insurance scheme in 1911. It was not that Belfast socialists had been persuaded to embrace Connolly's republicanism: the apparent inevitability of Home Rule, British Labour policy on Ireland, and apprehension about the exclusion of Ulster were the tipping points. Connolly's fear that partition would lead to a 'carnival of reaction' was exceptional only in its eloquence. The ILP in Belfast was driven to ground during the third Home Rule crisis. Socialists teetered between the logic of anti-partitionism and the overwhelming realities confronting them. By 1913 they had abandoned the ILP (of Ireland), and 'It had virtually no influence [in Belfast], least of all in the labour-trade union movement'.[75]

Circumstances improved as constitutional issues were overtaken by wartime conditions. An Ulster Socialist Party existed in 1915 and hosted an anti-war lecture from suffragette Margaret McCoubrey. Belfast's two ILP branches enjoyed a resurgence in 1917, organising over 40 open air propaganda meetings that summer.[76] In November they considered contesting the next elections, and in April 1918 the trades council convened a conference of 120 delegates from affiliates and the ILP to form the Belfast LRC. Its claim to represent 50,000 workers was fanciful – the trades council's membership was much lower – but implies it had the backing of a broad range of unions.[77] The drift towards Home Rule continued. When the British government invited the trades councils of Dublin, Belfast, and Cork, to take a seat each in the Irish Convention, Dublin and Cork spurned the offer, and the ITUC executive decided not to seek a presence. Belfast accepted, and sent Henry Whitley. As seven of the 95 seats were allocated to Labour, the government simply picked six other Labour men: Hanna, who was designated as representing 'Labour (Shipyards)', Thomas Lundon, MP, who was designated 'Labour (Land and Labour Association)', and four genuine trade unionists, Charles McKay, chairman of the FEST in Belfast, Robert Waugh, an official of the ASCJ, representing the Belfast and District Building Trades Federation, James McCarron, a Derry tailor, a Redmondite, and former ITUC president, and John Murphy, a relatively obscure Dublin railwayman. Whitley, Waugh, McKay, McCarron, and Murphy submitted their own minority report, favouring Home Rule, something Whitley and Waugh had formerly opposed.[78] After the conclusion of the Irish Convention, Unionist trade unionists in Belfast countered with a delegation to London, and meetings of members of the Boilermakers' Society and the NAUL in Harland and Wolff passed resolutions emphatically objecting to Home Rule.[79]

Belfast acted unilaterally when the ITUC withdrew from the 1918 general election. Davy Campbell protested that the withdrawal would 'give a walkover to the Conservative crowd in the North'.[80] In a vigorous campaign, featuring an organ recital in the Ulster Hall, the LRC ran four candidates; three were Home Rulers. Doing their best to foreground bread and butter issues and avoid 'politics', the real Labourites polled a respectable average of 22 per cent of the vote in predominantly Protestant constituencies. None enjoyed the luxury of a straight fight against the Unionists, having to compete with Sinn Féiners too. Waugh, a reluctant Home Ruler, did best in Victoria, with 26 per cent of the poll. James Freeland, Irish organiser of the ASE and a quiet anti-Home Ruler, did worst in Cromac, with 17 per cent. Sam Kyle, an official of the Workers' Union and a friend of Connolly, polled 23 per cent in Shankill and Samuel Porter, BL, won 21 per cent in Pottinger. Both were ILP'ers. As a law student, Porter had had a passing connection with Connolly's Irish Socialist Republican Party and identified publicly with the Liberals during the third Home Rule crisis. On the hustings, he openly favoured dominion Home Rule.[81] Arguably, the LRC was still Walkerite at heart. In 1919 it applied to join the British Labour Party, only to be told to redirect its enquiries to the Irish Labour Party, just as Irish Labour was telling prospective Irish branches cross-channel to join the British Labour Party. The LRC then opted to go solo as the Belfast Labour Party, retaining its structure as an umbrella for trade unions and the ILP.[82] But for all its Walkerism, Belfast Labour had come to a consensus on Home Rule as a better alternative than partition.

Another consolation from the general election was that despite making much of being 'Labour', and winning three seats, the UULA failed to gain credibility as a bona fide Labour body. As early as March 1919, Sam McGuffin, UULA MP for Shankill, was deposed as president of the Belfast ASE Literary Society for breaking his promise to vote with the British Labour Party at Westminster, an ominous development according to William Lorimer, a rare ILP defector to the UULA, 'knowing the political and theological composition of the Society'.[83] With the promise of a big shift to the left after the war, the future was looking bright for Baird and his fellow Labourites.

CHAPTER 2

The 44

Work for the night is coming
When man's work is o'er.
But NOW'S the time to work, boys,
To get the 'forty-four'.

Workers' Bulletin, 3 February 1919.

James Baird emerged from the obscurity of his union branch in 1918 as a shopfloor leader in a movement of engineering and shipbuilding workers that was gathering pace throughout the UK. The cost of living had risen significantly during the war, storing up class tensions against the farmers, shopkeepers, and employers who were felt to be doing well out of the war economy. After a delay, earnings in shipyards too began to rise, especially after December 1916, when the government took control of shipbuilding and the railways in Ireland. In the former, normal industrial relations were suspended, and wages were set by a Committee of Production, which was more generous in the payment of war bonuses. In consequence, with growing fear of a slump, a glut of ships, and a surfeit of labour at the end of the war, the movement's emphasis fell on shorter hours. Currently, the week was 54 hours, from 6.30am until 5.30pm Monday to Fridays, with a break for breakfast at 8am or 8.30am and a dinner break from 12.40pm to 1.20pm. Saturday was a half-day, stretching from 6am until noon, with the usual stop for breakfast. The shorter hours movement was an unusual instance of rank-and-file action in Belfast. There were various reasons for membership moderation. With no conscription and a very small munitions industry – employing a mere 2,169 persons by the armistice – the war had brought virtually no dilution or restructuring of the labour force in Irish engineering and shipbuilding of the kind that produced a powerful shopsteward movement in Britain.[1] Grade distinctions remained important. Craftsmen were particularly annoyed that post-1916 war bonuses were flat across the board, eroding the differential with labourers. The exclusion of engineers from a special award for all skilled time-workers in 1917 led to the only serious wartime strike in the Belfast yards. How important the Conservative politics of the Islandmen were, is harder to determine. As a constraint, it remained weakest on wage militancy and strongest on political radicalism, but if militancy and radicalism were not the same, they were not unconnected. Loyalty remained part of the yardmen's self-image. James Freeland boasted to the Ministry of Munitions that they 'have been the most law-abiding workmen that you have in the British Isles,' though the better to make his case for defusing the rising militancy in the ASE.[2] What is clear is that there was no equivalent to the shopstewards' movement on the Clyde, and the FEST retained its traditional grip on industrial relations. The 44 hours strike especially showed that there would be no Red Laganside to match Red Clydeside. Baird wondered why, and it would turn him from a faithful functionary of the Boilermakers' Society to a socialist critic of British trade unionism generally.

THE STRIKE

In the summer of 1918, the Boilermakers' Society requested the Engineering Employers' Federation to introduce a 44-hour week on the return of peace. In Belfast, a rank-and-file strand in the process was initiated in July when 'a few' shipyard workers formed a committee, began a propaganda campaign, and threatened a strike.[3] Officials of the Belfast district committee of the FEST were invited to a meeting in the Ulster Hall on 21 August, chaired by Baird.[4] With the crowd spilling out onto the street, Baird proposed they demand a 44-hour week, 8.30am to 5.30pm with an hour for dinner, Monday to Friday, and an 8.30am to 12.30pm day on Saturdays. Implying a broader vision, he went on: 'They have determined that in future workers must have ample leisure to enable them to take an active interest in all that concerns the welfare of their country. They were no longer content to be mere producers.' By a large majority the meeting amended the proposal to demand a 44-hour week, with no work on Saturday. It was also agreed to let matters be until the end of the war. At this point it was felt that with the failure of its 'spring offensive' Germany's defeat was inevitable, but 'the Huns' could hold out for another year. A collection was made to defray expenses, with any surplus to go to Ulster prisoners of war. Baird would later rue the temporizing, but at the time he was delighted with the outcome. His committee then left matters to the FEST. The FEST interviewed employers in Belfast and decided to await the outcome of negotiations in Britain.[5]

One week after the armistice, on 19 November, the FEST agreed to put the British Engineering Employers' Federation offer of a 47-hour week to a ballot. Baird later implied that his colleagues were pressing for action and telling the FEST's Belfast committee to 'get on or get out'.[6] Both parties agreed to hold a meeting in the Ulster Hall on 5 December, just after the close of nominations for the forthcoming general election. All candidates were invited to attend, and the presence of Sir Edward Carson on the platform indicated the meeting's importance. From the chair, Baird made an appeal, common at trade union rallies in Ulster, to avoid politics: 'The alarm clock which aroused them from dreamland knew no politics. (Applause). The idea of a forty-four hours' week was worth striving for, and, if necessary, worth fighting for. (Applause)'. Of course, by 'politics' was meant the constitutional question, and the meeting patently reflected the peculiarities of the Belfast shipyards. The Nationalist and Sinn Féin runners in the forthcoming general election stayed away, and those present included two of the three UULA nominees. Also present were three of the four LRC candidates.[7] After the proceedings opened with a rendition of 'God Save the King', Carson was received with loud cheers, according to the Unionist *Belfast News-Letter*, and some heckling, according to the nationalist *Irish News*. He spoke ambivalently, endorsing the 44 hours demand in principle, but counselling Belfast to accept whatever was agreed in Britain.[8] The Unionist Party would follow Carson's lead in treading delicately between tepid support for the men and uneasiness about their tactics. The general election confirmed that attitudes had shifted in Belfast, if not decisively. Two greater uncertainties introduced into the political equation were the election of the three UULA men, and the Sinn Féin landslide in the south. Labour's attention shifted back to the industrial question.

On 24 December the Employers' Federation and the FEST agreed to a 47-hour week from 1 January. In Belfast, the day would start at 8.10am and run to 5.20pm, with a dinner break from 12.40pm to 1.20pm. Saturday work would run from 8.10am to 12.40pm, with no break. In the Boilermakers' poll, more than two-thirds rejected the deal, but in the FEST generally, roughly the same fraction of voters accepted it.[9] The Belfast FEST decided on a local ballot for unofficial action. In the meantime it sent Baird, as a representative of the Boilermakers, and two others from the ASE and the Friendly Society of Operative Iron Moulders, to consult with shopstewards in Glasgow who were arguing over their own objective. The shopsteward-dominated and unofficial Clyde Workers' Committee was demanding a strike for a 30-hour week, whereas the Glasgow FEST favoured action for a 40 hour week, a target the Belfastmen thought still too ambitious.[10] Eventually the Committee would row in behind the FEST for the sake of unity.[11]

Voting in Belfast took place on 14 January, and Baird was one of four speakers to address a preliminary rally in Donegall Place. At noon, work had stopped in the shipyards and engineering shops. While many hurried home to change into 'holiday attire' or went straight to vote, over 20,000 marched in their dongarees through the high streets, with union banners and placards, and flute bands setting aside 'party' tunes for 'It's far too airly in the morning'. Police kept the crowd outside the City Hall grounds, where the flora was still recovering from the armistice celebrations. From the platform on a lorry, Baird told them the time for talking was over, it was time for action. It was not rhetorical. There was not much to be said; the outcome was a foregone conclusion. The men then dispersed to their various union halls to vote. Already the cosy connection between the unions and the authorities was evident. The ballot boxes were provided by the Corporation and were the same as those used in the recent general election. The results were announced at 9.30pm. Asked if they favoured acceptance of the employers' offer of a 47-hour week, 1,184 workers ticked 'yes', and 13,508 ticked 'no'; 20,225 then voted for 'drastic action in the way of an unofficial strike' and 558 voted against. Amidst the euphoria, the *News-Letter* noted that just 50 per cent of those concerned had voted and the movement was not as strong as it appeared.[12] Work resumed next morning.

The strike began on 25 January and involved 26 unions, up to 40,000 workers directly, 20,000 indirectly, and 44 businesses including the shipyards, the town engineering shops, linen mills, and the Belfast Ropeworks. Soon the trouble spread to municipal employees and stopped the trams. In some respects authority passed from City Hall to the general strike committee (GSC) in the Artizans' Hall in Garfield Street. Its control of gas, water, and electricity supplies gave it an administrative authority and the establishment of a permit system, enforced by 2,500 official pickets, to allow for essential services, led journalists to refer to the 'Belfast Soviet'. The GSC was an elaborate affair, 150 strong, with sub-committees on finance, organisation, picketing, the press, and entertainment. As newspapers shut down or curtailed their production, the GSC published its own *Workers' Bulletin*. With copies priced at 1d. each, 18 issues were printed between 25 January and 19 February.[13] Ian Macpherson, Chief Secretary for Ireland, warned that the 'Soviet Committee', as he called the GSC, 'had received 47 applications from small traders for permission to use light'.[14]

Baird's role on the GSC is unclear. He was mentioned just once in the *Workers' Bulletin*, as rapporteur to Belfast linen and pieceworkers on a conference in London on 3 February.[15] This in itself was the editorial practice. Far from boosting their champions and giving them personalities with which the rank and file could identify, as was usual in a strike, the

Bulletin said little on the men and activity of the self-effacing GSC, most likely to conceal their politics or anything else which could be construed as anti-Unionist. The *Bulletin's* staff too remained anonymous. The tactic did not go unnoticed. 'Some of the strongest public advocates of the 44-hour movement when it commenced last summer are – probably by their own desire – rather in the background now', observed the *Northern Whig*.[16] The *Whig*'s editor, Unionist MP Robert Lynn, believed 'the Church of Rome' to be behind all of Ulster's troubles and saw the Labour left as its useful idiot.[17] Seeking to lift the GSC's veil, he spotted Baird as one attempting to theorize what was happening and willing to go public on it. The *Whig*, which had its own power supply and was able to continue regardless, listed him on 8 February as one of 14 most prominent strike leaders. A Unionist councillor also singled out Baird and denounced him as a syndicalist. Unfazed, Baird published a letter on 11 February defending the 'hold-up theory', as Lynn called it, i.e. ensuring the strike 'held up' the community through maximum inconvenience. Baird argued that trade unionism was evolving towards 'one big union' which would use strikes strategically as a 'citizen army' to win workers' control of industry. But when a *Whig* editorial accused him of preaching class war, he denied it and denied being a member of the GSC.[18] Morgan concludes that as soon as he emerged as the strike's foremost socialist and militant, he was removed from the GSC.[19]

It was a delicate time for moderates. Europe was still in the melting pot. Aside from the Bolshevik revolution and the possibility of more revolutions in Germany and elsewhere in central Europe, peace talks had opened in Paris in January, and it was widely believed that there would have to be a pay-back for Labour in the eventual settlement. It would come, anticlimactically, in Chapter XIII of the Treaty of Versailles, which set up the International Labour Organisation. Meanwhile, the confidential *Press Review* of the general staff of the American Expeditionary Force noted in its digest of news of Britain:

> An editorial in the *Morning News*, February 1, on the subject of strikes, deserved special notice because of its emphatic references to the leaders of the movement. 'We hope the government and the country are under no illusion about what is happening in Glasgow and Belfast. It is not merely an industrial movement; it is an attempt at revolution. The leaders are not recognized trade union leaders; some of them are not even British workingmen. The bell-wether in the Glasgow upheaval is a Jewish tailor named Shinwell; in the Belfast strike Shinwell's counterpart is one Simon Greenspon, a Jew of Russian descent. These two are the Trotskys of Belfast and Glasgow...[20]

Nor was the alarm confined to the popular end of the Tory press. *The Times* 'believed that an attempt was being made to start the 'class war'...The men on strike in Belfast and Glasgow are the unconscious instruments of a planned campaign, drawn up by 'intellectuals' in the background, who desire to emulate Lenin and Trotsky and the Spartacist leaders in Germany'.[21]

Simon Wolfe Greenspon was indeed one of a small knot of radicals attempting to link the dispute with revolution and urging solidarity with workers in the rest of Ireland. Militants thought he did 'great work' during the strike.[22] Greenspon was born in Dublin, and was chairman of Belfast's central branch of the Electrical Trades Union. He had worked since the war years, at least, as an electrician on Queen's Island. As a Jew, he attracted attention. The *Church of Ireland Gazette* reported 'a Russian Jew born in Dublin and educated in London,' telling workers outside the electricity station that 'there are no Papishes in this movement; there are no Orangemen; there are no Unionists; we are all plain working men'. The *Gazette* went so far as to blame him for the strike: 'The Russian Jew...along with his *Sinn Féin* friends has succeeded in dragging the Belfast workingman into a terrible mess'.[23] Dawson Bates told Carson of workers' resentment 'at men like the Russian Jew being brought from Dublin to teach Belfast men their business', and he may have been the model for 'A Jew in Gaelic clothing' in *Tales of the RIC*, a collection of yarns about life during the War of Independence.[24] Two other protagonists in the circle were Jack Hedley and Charles O'Meagher. 'Shanghai' Hedley, originally from Yorkshire and in Belfast as a member of the Workers' Union, was an inveterate roving agitator, who would accumulate an extraordinary curriculum vitae. Politics would lead to his imprisonment for separate offences in 1919, 1920, and 1921. His wife, Bella Sarah, was a doughty accomplice.[25] O'Meagher, a Dubliner, had deserted from the army. Trading as O'Mahon, O'Hagan, and Meehan, respectively, the trio were involved in three strike meetings in front of the City Hall. At their third meeting, Hedley was challenged by a leader of the FEST and the crowd turned against him, allowing two uniformed tars and a silver badge man (a wounded, discharged soldier) to bundle him off the platform amid heckles against 'Bolshevism' and Sinn Féin. 'O'Hagan and his pals' were then repudiated by FEST and GSC leaders, and abandoned their efforts to influence the strike. Following the establishment of the Communist International, they formed the Revolutionary Socialist Party of Ireland.[26]

The *Belfast News-Letter* shared the outlook of the British press about the motivation of the workers' leaders, describing the stoppage as 'anarchic socialism', but added a local twist: 'There is more than trade unionism and the desire for shorter hours in this situation...The threat to paralyse the public services if carried out will rejoice the heart of Sinn Féin and will play most powerfully into its hands'.[27] The Unionist hierarchy shared the *News-*

Letter's concerns. Dawson Bates told Sir James Craig on 1 February: 'The aim of Sinn Féin is to let matters drift on in Belfast until conditions arise in which the men would be so embittered with the authorities that they would join hands in a universal strike for the whole of Ireland'.[28] Unionists wanted an end to the strike as quickly as possible, but were reluctant to confront the strikers, and careful to follow Carson's lead in presenting themselves as sympathetic to the men and understanding of the issue at heart.

In some respects, the GSC was as ambiguous in policy as the Unionist Party. The *Workers' Bulletin* counselled moderation and wrote about the need for workers' control.[29] The GSC disavowed any ambition to disrupt and hoped that widespread inconvenience would force a quick settlement. On politics, however, the GSC was more straightforward than the *Workers' Bulletin*, making plain that it wanted nothing to do with the likes of 'O'Hagan' and that it was determined to keep the strike parochial and a-political. Even Belfast trades council was kept out of the picture. Whereas the ASE had sought the aid of the council in the lockout of 1897 and the ASCJ sought the council's help during their long strike in 1899–1900, the GSC ignored the council.[30] The traditional suspicions of shipyard craft unions were reinforced by the council's involvement with the anti-conscription campaign. Numbers affiliated by the council to the ITUC, a rough indication of strength, actually fell from 15,000 in 1919 to 10,000 in 1920.[31] Though the Orange Order and the UULA did not 'take sides' in the dispute, two of the 14 strike leaders identified by the *Northern Whig*, Bob Weir, a machinist in Harland and Wolff, and Billy Grant, an official of the Ship Constructive and Shipwrights' Association, were UULA activists. Grant would later become Minister of Health at Stormont. His parliamentary secretary, the future Prime Minister Terence O'Neill, described him as 'a typical Belfast Protestant working man, strongly anti-Catholic, but decent'.[32]

During the first two weeks, the GSC hoped the strike would spark action cross-channel. John Milan, a Londoner recently appointed organiser of the Electrical Trades Union in Belfast, was particularly active in canvassing districts in England and Scotland, and gave speeches hinting of 'further great developments' ahead.[33] But the haggling continued, with the exception of Glasgow, where the FEST struck on 27 January. This too would present problems for the GSC. Glasgow was more avowedly radical than Belfast, and the government feared nothing less than revolution on Clydeside. After the 'Battle of George Square' on 31 January, which saw fighting between strikers and police in central Glasgow, the GSC dissociated itself from the Scottish dispute and affirmed that 'They in Belfast were determined they would be an object lesson to the world as to how a strike should be conducted...'.[34] Extending the strike in Ireland, or nationalist Ireland, at least, was more problematic for a GSC determined to avoid any association, or accusation of association, with 'politics'. The ITUC sent a 'telegram of encouragement' on the outbreak of the dispute. No reply was received.[35] When Denis Houston, the ITGWU's Belfast organiser, offered his union's services, the GSC pleaded that there were five transport unions in the city and inter-union rivalry would prevent them from taking sympathetic action. Nor did the GSC seek to raise funds to sustain the dispute.[36] In Derry, FEST officials invited all workers to the Guildhall on 3 February to discuss their response. Shy of asking bluntly for a sympathetic strike, they proposed that Derry unions levy members to help Belfast and notice all local employers for a 44-hour week by 1 May. When Thomas Cassidy rose to speak his presence was challenged, and he said he was there as 'a worker in Derry'. In fact, Cassidy was chairman of the ITUC executive. Cassidy argued that action had to be national, and pointed out that a conference was due in Dublin on 8 February to discuss the formation of an all-Ireland hours and wages movement. After lively exchanges, the meeting adopted an amendment that Derry workers be balloted on a 44-hours movement.[37]

The ITUC had circularised affiliates on 30 January with a call to a national conference to demand a working week of 44 hours, a wage increase of at least 150 per cent on pre-war rates, and a minimum wage of 50s. per week. The circular's invocation of Pope Leo XIII, author of *Rerum Novarum*, the first papal encyclical on the labour question, was not calculated to charm the black squad, and the unions in Belfast shipbuilding and engineering largely ignored the conference. In its only discussion of events in Belfast, the ITUC executive agreed on 7 February to 'that a resolution congratulating the workers of Belfast on their fight for a 44-hour week s[houl]d be moved at the conference' and that they be assured of 'hearty support…moral and financial'. A collection among delegates raised £14.5s. and the conference agreed 'with acclamation' on an unprecedented levy of 1s. per week on all workers for the GSC's fighting fund. The *Workers' Bulletin* noted the conference tersely, without reporting its gestures to Belfast. 'The Irish workers have been slow in making a start,' wrote the *Bulletin*, as if they were foreigners, 'but once they begin to go there will be no stopping them'. Yet the same issue featured another article delicately encouraging Belfast to embrace north-south solidarity.

> The workers of the rest of Ireland do not want to dictate to the Belfast workers as to what should be done. Neither to they wish to take any action likely to prejudice the cause of their Belfast brethren, but if help is required, then Belfast has only to give the word. As said to me by prominent Labour leaders in other centres in Ireland, 'Does anyone imagine that we would stand idly by whilst the women and children of our Belfast fellow workers were likely to suffer the pangs of hunger and distress?'[38]

Though there were reports of communications between the FEST and Dublin trades council, and the GSC proposed to respond to the ITUC offers, it then changed its mind. The levy was never applied, but the Congress accounts for 1919 included a Belfast strike fund with £50, in addition to the 'substantial sum' raised in the collection.[39]

The unusual relationship between the metal trades and the authorities was evident in the inscription of 300 strikers as special constables after crowds had damaged property in Belfast city centre. The RIC paid tribute to the GSC's effectiveness in eradicating the influence of revolutionary tourists, lured to Belfast by the strike.[40] The Viceroy in Dublin, the blimpish Sir John French, was not so sure. Alarmed at the contagion of 'Bolshevism' and the prospect of Sinn Féin winning Protestant support through it, Dublin Castle sent in troops on Saturday 14 February to take over the gasworks and electricity station. On Sunday, trams began to trundle again. The GSC accepted that the strike was crumbling, the Glasgow strike had collapsed on 10 February, and hopes of cross-channel support had evaporated. The GSC recommended a return to work. The strongest opposition came from within the ASE and the Boilermakers.[41] Baird complained that the *Workers' Bulletin* was not allowed to 'give a lead against the offer'.[42]

BEARDING THE VOICE

Soon after the Ulster Hall meeting in August 1918, Baird began to engage with the *Voice of Labour*. The *Voice* was owned by a co-operative called the Irish Labour Press and nominally served the entire movement. In practice it reflected the views of the ITGWU, relied heavily on 'organised salesmanship' in the expanding network of ITGWU branches, and was edited by an ITGWU officer, Cathal O'Shannon, an enthusiastic Gaeilgeor and republican as well as a self-styled 'Irish Bolshevik'. An ardent feminist too, O'Shannon secretly wrote the election address of Winifred Carney, the Sinn Féin candidate in Belfast Victoria in the 1918 general election and printed it in the *Voice*.[43] A motion of support for the paper at the ITUC annual conference in August 1918 encountered criticism from delegates of British-based unions. O'Shannon was happy to respond to complaints about the lack of northern coverage by Councillor William Logue, Derry trades council. Raised in Draperstown, County Derry, a scholarship boy in St Columb's College, Derry, and an ITGWU official in Belfast in 1913, he was keen to embrace his native province and had cultivated contacts in the Belfast ILP. Fraternal contacts with Belfast's ILP'ers were nurtured also through the Socialist Party of Ireland, in which O'Shannon was a linchpin.[44] As Logue conceded, the problem had its roots in northern indifference to Dublin, and O'Shannon sought to stir a response with provocative references to shipyard workers as 'the black squad' and the UULA as 'Orange Bolshies'. 'Workers and the 'south and west'', he opined, trailing his coat across the front page:

> have long been accustomed to think of Belfast as an industrial Oxford – the home of lost causes, unreasoning conservatism, political and social, with a hopelessly parochial outlook. Their loyalty to trade unionism has been unquestioned, but they have entertained, long after the British worker had abandoned it, the view of trade unionism as a merely protective instrument.

Logue responded, saying that trade unionism in Ulster had 'in large measure succeeded', and could compare favourably with any part of the United Kingdom. He acknowledged that in politics the picture was not so bright due to northern 'suspicions', but was optimistic that 'we are gradually emerging into that position when we fully realise our strength'. The *Voice* remained sceptical, though it welcomed the shorter hours movement and told the shipyard unions to apply their proposed regime unilaterally and immediately.[45]

Baird was one of the few other northerners to join the debate. Emphasising that Ulster opposition to Home Rule was based on fear of 'Rome rule', he suggested that public control of education would go some way to assuaging Unionist concerns, and anticipated 'some sort of 'settlement' of the Home Rule question...in the not distant future'. Once Home Rule was 'out of the way', Ulster would quickly become 'the most democratic province in Ireland'. Another issue dividing the north and south was that of the so-called 'English Unions' which were not 'any more English than Irish'. In a jibe at O'Shannon's ITGWU, he ventured that Irish unions of recent vintage might be less hasty to claim superiority over 'that sturdy [trade] Unionism which took root three quarters of a century ago in Belfast...'. Baird returned to the theme of Home Rule and Rome rule in the *Voice* in October, citing the suppression of the weekly review *Peasant* in 1910 and asking how a people could demand self-determination and be 'too cowardly' to protest against clerical interference in secular affairs?[46] The Catholic primate Michael Cardinal Logue had condemned the *Peasant* for discussing public control of education, causing the proprietors to discontinue it. Its editor, W. P. Ryan, weary of being denounced as a socialist, packed his bags for London and began work with the *Daily Herald*. Baird's 'bolt', as O'Shannon styled it, drew a varied response. Ryan, a regular Irish language contributor to the *Voice*, assured Baird that there had been protests, a Cork correspondent denounced him as an 'imperialistic shipwright', and two Queen's University professors wrote to oppose public control of education. O'Shannon could not resist heading the debate 'Two professors and a boilermaker'.[47]

The *Voice of Labour* applauded the 44 hours strike as an encouraging sign of militancy with no illusions as to its political ramifications. 'The workers of Belfast are not revolutionary', wrote O'Shannon, 'We know that well, for we have tried, and failed, to make them so'.[48] Baird responded with a letter to the *Voice* on 22 February, arguing that for the likely prospect of lengthy 'industrial warfare', workers needed strategic preparation in the form of co-operatives to guarantee supplies and, above all, 'One Big Union'. Their ultimate aim should be to capture the machinery of state. It was just the kind of syndicalist language beloved of the *Voice*. On 8 March he went further in a front-page open letter to the GSC. It amounted to a withering denunciation of the FEST for restraining the rank and file since July 1918 and of the GSC for making no appeal for financial assistance, refusing offers of help from the ITGWU, and accepting an outcome that fell short of what had been promised. In the ensuing debate, Sam Haslett, the GSC's watchful eye on the *Workers' Bulletin*, dismissed the claims as irrelevant, as all offers of aid fell far short of the £50,000 weekly that would have been needed to sustain the strike. Corroborating Baird's poor opinion of the leadership, he went on: 'No one knowing the Belfast workers would assert that they would face the distress with soup kitchens, etc, for a long period over the fight for one half hour a day'. However, William Lorimer, a former ILP'er who would later join the Unionist Party, argued that the provenance of assistance had been a stumbling block, contending that the craft unions found the ITGWU's industrial unionism unacceptable and citing an instance where a £100 donation had required 'a full-fledged debate' as the donor had 'rejoiced at the blending of orange and green'. Milan struck what would become the official Labour view of events, applauding the solidarity shown and saying the GSC had done the best it could in the absence of support cross-channel.[49] The annual report of the ITUC blamed the collapse of the strike on 'the failure of the shipyard workers in England and Scotland to act with similar energy and unanimity'. Far from being miffed by the GSC's snubs, delegates to the annual congress that August, of whom a mere 17 out of 226 were from Belfast, largely insisted that the strike was a moral victory and had brought positive results.[50]

Baird undertook one final bid for higher office in his union that summer, standing for the executive council in its no.2 district, which covered Ireland and north-west England. His chief opponent was the incumbent James Bell, from Ballymacarrett no.2 lodge. Baird gleaned a respectable tally in the Belfast district, but failed to carry more than his own branch, and as he put it himself in a gracious letter to the Boilermakers' *Monthly Report*, Bell's victory was decisive.[51]

CHAPTER 3

The Dongarees

The truth is, Baird is a bit of a jealous chap and likes to be the star...

Peter Keating on Baird.[1]

In January 1920 James Baird was elected to Belfast Corporation for the Belfast Labour Party. No local elections had been held since 1914, and they were further delayed after the First World War to allow for the introduction of a new electoral system. The Local Government (Ireland) Act of June 1919 provided for municipal and Urban District Council elections to be held under proportional representation. Unionists alone protested, ironically as the British government hoped proportional representation would avoid another Sinn Féin landslide like that in the 1918 general election. The Belfast franchise was much increased, from 73,405 in 1914, to 135,538, or about 32 per cent of the city's population.[2] The elections marked the high tide of the post-war radicalism in Belfast. They were the last time the trades council would engage in municipal politics.

Nationally, results of the local elections were dramatic. On a 70 per cent turnout, Labour did well throughout Ireland, winning 394 seats to 550 for Sinn Féin, 238 for the Nationalists, and 355 for the Unionist Party. Labour was still a collection of unions and trades councils rather than a cohesive machine. The Labour programme had been settled at a two-day conference of trades councils in Dublin's Mansion House on 24–5 October 1919. Labour candidates were to be approved by 'legitimate' Labour bodies and be pledge-bound to act as a party under trades council direction, if elected. Confined to the six county boroughs in 1914, trades councils sprang up in most towns after 1917. There were 15 by 1918 and 46 by 1921.[3] Of 38 trades councils affiliated to the ITUC over 1919–20, seven were in Ulster, at Belfast, Cavan, Derry, Enniskillen, Monaghan, Newry, and Omagh. The northern connection with Congress was still tenuous. Some councils, like that in Strabane, were not affiliated, and only Belfast and Omagh sent delegates to the local elections convention. Belfast was also represented by Dawson Gordon as a member of the ITUC executive.[4] Derry trades council, alone among affiliates, was noted as 'unrepresented without valid reason', and, uniquely among Irish cities, it ultimately fielded no Labour candidates at all. Some Derry trades council activists stood for the Nationalists and others for Sinn Féin, while the local Unionist Party ran four UULA men. There were difficulties too with bringing the nomination of all Labour candidates under trades council control in Cork, Limerick, Wexford, and Dublin, as well as Belfast. Nonetheless, it was a start to the creation of a functioning all-Ireland party and the results were promising. The ITUC looked forward to another conference to develop 'a common line of activity'.[5] Across Ulster, Labour won 19.8 per cent of the first preferences, compared with 14.9 per cent for the Nationalists, 8.9 per cent for Sinn Féin, and 52.6 per cent for the Unionists.[6] Aside from the surge in the Labour vote, Unionists were uneasy about the open collusion between Labour and republicans in places like Cork. From the *Irish Times* to Sinn Féin's *Irish Bulletin*, the press remarked on how the elections undermined the Unionist claim to represent Ulster and the case for partition. Never known for understatement, the ITGWU's *Watchword of Labour* declared: 'As Labour stands solidly with Sinn Féin on the national question, the election really means that the Empire is in danger and with it the whole capitalist system'.[7]

It was cold comfort to Unionists that Labour in Ulster was more likely to distance itself from orange and green. Dawson Bates assured Carson that the results 'look worse than they really are', and did not mean 'any change whatever in the feeling of the people in regard to Home Rule'.[8] The fault, he believed, lay with proportional representation. It is true that the local Labour victories were based on bread and butter issues, notably housing, open spaces for children, swimming baths, electricity, the trams, and the cost of food and fuel. But the political leadership of Labour could see beyond to the constitutional implications, and was embracing Home Rule. Unionism seemed to be losing the battle to direct the working class on questions other than the constitution. As the *News-Letter* conceded, 'there is something wrong with Unionist Labour...Big questions of municipal enterprise...bulked large in this election. These questions had been much exploited by Socialist Labour from an extreme class point of view...'.[9]

'HAMMERING AT THE GATES IN ULSTER'[10]

The outgoing Belfast Corporation consisted of 52 Unionists and eight Nationalists – all from the Falls – numbers that had rarely varied since the introduction of democratic local government in 1899. Belfast Labour had not been a significant factor in local politics since the LRC's wipe-out on the council in 1907.

3.1 *Local elections in Belfast, January 1920*

	Number of candidates	Votes	% vote	Seats won
Unionist	47	40,907	46.0	29
UULA	8	4,699	5.3	6
Independent Unionist	5	4,167	4.7	2
Belfast Labour Party	22	12,768	14.3	10
NAUL	3	1,138	1.3	-
Independent Labour	10	3,007	3.4	2
Nationalist	16	10,758	12.0	5
Sinn Féin	12	7,120	8.0	5
Independent	20	4,467	5.0	1
Total		89,031		

Source: Alec Wilson, *PR Urban Elections in Ulster, 1920* (London, 1972), pp.14, 46.

The turnout in 1920 was a little below average at just under 66 per cent. Wilson's meticulous study of the elections for the Ulster Extension Committee of the Proportional Representation Society of Ireland, a voluntary and non-partisan body, reckoned that Catholics accounted for 20 per cent of the vote, and that 'Protestants voted, to the number of at least 10,000, for Labour instead of for Unionist candidates'. He also classed Labour as a 'mainly Protestant' party. Measuring the results against those in the 1918 general election, Wilson calculated that almost 20 per cent of Catholic voters had switched first preferences from Nationalist or Sinn Féin to Labour in the Falls, but there was no evidence of a sizable switch elsewhere. Sinn Féin publications were banned at the time, and the nationalist press was solidly anti-republican. However, there were wards where a high level of Nationalist transfers helped Labour to a second seat.[11]

The Belfast Labour Party contested all wards. Seven of its candidates were ILP'ers, two, Denis Houston, Belfast organiser of the ITGWU, and Davy Campbell, were nominated by the trades council, and the others were proposed by their trade unions.[12] Both Labour candidates were successful in Ormeau and took two of the six seats with 18 per cent of the vote. Campbell would become leader of the Labour group of councillors. Baird polled a respectable 802 first preferences. Attracting few transfers in the early counts, he was elected on the 10th count to the last of the six seats with substantial transfers from a Nationalist, and without reaching the quota.[13] His candidature was commended by temperance societies and the Ulster Society for the Prevention of Cruelty to Animals, which was lobbying for abattoir reform.[14]

Labour seemed to have contained the Orange threat. In addition to the open rivalry of the Unionist Party and the UULA, there were oblique challenges, chiefly from the NAUL and the British Empire Union. Founded in 1916 out of the Anti-German Union, the British Empire Union turned its attention to combatting 'Bolsheviks' and Jews after the war. It was well connected in Belfast, with Edward Carson as a president and an office at 13 Donegall Square North. By mid-1920, its Belfast branch claimed 5,000 members.[15] With a proven capacity to organise mass rallies, its agents lobbied Labour Party candidates. Nineteen refused to answer their questionnaire, but three responded positively, as did three other independent labour candidates. The NAUL stood aside from the Labour Party and fielded its own slate of three candidates. All favoured the Empire Union. One of the three, Sam Bradley, became Irish District Secretary of the National Union of General and Municipal Workers in 1924. There were also calls during the election campaign for Protestant employers to dismiss 'disloyal' workers in retaliation for the war in the south.[16] Of those elected, the two Independent Labourites were Unionist on the Home Rule question, as was Alex Boyd. Boyd was often described as 'Labour'. A former Independent Orangeman, he had sat with Baird on Belfast trades council, and served as Big Jim Larkin's deputy in the 1907 dock strike. Alderman Boyd topped the poll in St Anne's ward, covering Sandy Row, with a whopping 1,627 first preferences. It typified the mixed message in the results. Labour did well, but so too did some loyalists like Boyd and the UULA men. Loyalism was not all about politics and sectarianism, it also fed on rank-and-file populism. For Robert McElborough, one of Boyd's campaign champions, the motivation was resentment of union officials serving their British masters rather than Ulster workers. Most of Boyd's surplus went to Labour's George Donaldson. Both Boyd and Donaldson would endorse the workplace expulsions in 1920.[17]

3.2 *The Labour group on Belfast City Council, 1920*

	Other affiliations	Ward
Belfast Labour Party		
Ald. G.M. Donaldson*	Operative Plumbers' and Domestic Engineers' Association	St Anne's
Ald. Sam Kyle*	Workers' Union, ILP	Shankill
James Baird	Boilermakers' Society, ILP	Ormeau
D. R. Campbell	National Union of Life Assurance Agents	Ormeau
Dawson Gordon*	Flax Roughers' and Yarn Spinners' Trade Union, ILP	Shankill
Denis Houston*	ITGWU	Falls
J. A. Kennedy	ASCJ	Victoria
J. S. Lawther	ILP	Duncairn
J. S. L. McKeag*	Workers' Union, ILP	Pottinger
Clarke Scott	Union of Post Office Workers	Woodvale
Independent Labour		
T. Kennedy	ASE	Cromac
J. Addis	ASE	Woodvale
Ald. Alderman *Full-time union official		

Source: *Watchword of Labour*, 31 January 1920; Alec Wilson, *PR Urban Elections in Ulster, 1920* (London, 1972), pp18–35.

Elsewhere in Ulster, Labour candidates won 8,566 first preferences out of 50,346, and took 93 out of 505 seats on the Urban District Councils. Derry of course, the largest local authority outside Belfast with 9,637 electors, had no Labour candidates though three successful Unionist councillors were identified with the UULA, and at least three Nationalist and two Sinn Féin councillors were involved with the trades council. No love was lost between Derry's Labour nationalists and the Unionists and their 'so-called Labour association'. The trades council too was hostile and outraged when the outgoing Corporation had allocated three of the five labour seats on the local War Pensions Committee to the UULA.[18] But in Belfast, things looked splendid and Baird would reflect wistfully on the achievement before the British Trades Union Congress (BTUC) in September 1921.

> ...the workers were becoming class conscious. We had organised a little Labour Party. We had fought elections. Of course we had been defeated, but we were still making progress. Two years ago we thought and believed that

the bad old days were gone forever. We thought we had the workers of Belfast united as workers and that never again would the employers divide us as in the olden days....[19]

THE MOST FAMOUS TROUSERS IN LABOUR HISTORY

Some of the Labour, Sinn Féin, and Nationalist representatives raised eyebrows at the inauguration of the new Corporation by attending without their robes. Baird trumped them all and acquired a notoriety as 'Dongaree Baird' by walking into the magnificent City Hall in his working clothes, his cap 'thrust in a side-pocket'. 'If self-respect and dignity', wrote the *Belfast News-Letter,* 'did not teach Mr Baird better, respect to [sic] the position to which he has been elected should have done so. It may be that Mr Baird prides himself on the figure he made. We suspect he does, for what is at the root of it but small vanity...'. The sensation was noted in Dublin too. 'The stuff to give 'em in Belfast Corporation. Baird's dongarees and Campbell's nomination shock old gang. Angry capitalist press calls for blood', ran the headline in the *Watchword of Labour,* which delighted too in the *News-Letter*'s grammatical error.[20] Sensitive to the suggestion that Baird was disrespecting an icon of Unionist pride, famously described as 'a wedding cake at a pauper's funeral', the ILP sprang to his defence. Party speakers at a Custom House steps rally in support of the moulders' strike devoted considerable attention to comments in the *News-Letter* and the *Belfast Telegraph.* Baird himself explained that he had just completed a two-hour shift on Queen's Island and had no time to change before the Corporation meeting at 11am. He also raised the issue in his maiden speech on the council, requesting that its meetings be held in the evening, to facilitate the attendance of workers. 'Were the resolution to be carried,' he pleaded, 'he would be able to remove the disgusting dongarees. He usually kept a second suit by him, and he would be able to go home and make a change'. The resolution was defeated, by 33-22 votes.[21]

It would not be the last time Baird sported his 'dongaree suit' in the City Hall, and the *News-Letter* complained that his 'little vanity in the matter of clothes is apparently bullet-proof'. Nor would it be the last time the *News-Letter* editorialised against him or the 'Labour-Socialists' as the *News-Letter* insisted on calling them.[22] The Custom House meeting produced more embarrassment in leading to the arrest of Greenspon for remarks about Soviet Russia and police corruption. Baird and other ILP'ers were cited in the court hearing. The RIC sergeant swore Greenspon caused the crowd to shout 'That's the stuff to give them, Simon. Shoot them. They are getting their touch in Thurles', which sounds an unlikely response from ILP'ers in east Belfast. Greenspon was bound over to keep the peace for 12 months.

The sureties were paid by Alderman Sam Kyle and Hugh Campbell. He was scarcely out of prison. Sentenced to six months in gaol for 'unlawful assembly', he had been released in December 1919 owing to his hunger strike for political status and the illness of his only child.[23]

At the inaugural Corporation meeting, Labour had nominated Davy Campbell for Lord Mayor, proposed symbolically by Kyle from the Shankill and Houston from the Falls, each district a by-word for loyalism and nationalism respectively. Houston, a Donegal man from Glenfin, opened his speech in Irish, amidst Unionist shouts of 'Order, order'. Confirming the Unionist perception of a Labour-Sinn Féin bloc, two Sinn Féin councillors also spoke *as Gaeilge*. The proposal was defeated 18-36. The five Sinn Féiners and three Nationalists voted with Labour. The two Independent Labourites abstained. Labour, Sinn Féin, and the Nationalists also proposed that the Lord Mayor be paid a salary.[24] Unionist antipathy was reinforced by Labour's refusal to condemn the assassination of the RIC's Assistant Commissioner in Dublin, Belfastman William Redmond. Labour felt 'condemnation' was too politically tinged a term, and proposed to offer 'condolences' instead.[25]

The Labour group became the official opposition and made its presence felt with speeches on every item on the agenda. Baird was elected to the improvement, law, public health, markets, electricity, and coal committees, having objected to a new system of selection for committees, designed, he claimed, to guarantee Unionist Party control on all of them.[26] He also took a lively interest in the provision of better tramway services for shipyard workers, the wages of municipal employees, and housing. Housing had become a major issue in local politics. Housebuilding had stopped during the world war, as thousands were being drawn into the city in search of work in the booming war industries. After the war, the Unionist city fathers, many with their own property interests, were slow to act. Various figures, often exaggerated, were thrown back and forth by the antagonists. According to the census, the number of families living in one room in the city rose from 448 in 1911 to 2,682 in 1926. Ten thousand homes were needed, said Baird, and if he had his way, he would have the Corporation acquire land, quarries, lime-kilns, and all the materials necessary for housing construction. The Unionist councillors laughed, but the galleries applauded.[27] Labour claimed some success in having houses built by direct labour at £200 less per unit than those erected by contract.[28]

Baird quickly caught the attention of journalist William Forbes Patterson. Hailing from a Derry Presbyterian and Unionist family, Forbes Patterson had become a leading intellectual in Belfast nationalist circles, and brought out a paper, the *Northern Democrat*, to appeal to Protestant workers. In April, he sent two documents to Dáil Éireann, dealing with the military and the political situation, respectively. The first noted the superior firepower of loyalists and advised that Sinn Féin would not be able to combat a pogrom.[29] The second report mixed the age-old optimism that socialism would transcend sectarian divisions with a more realistic recognition of the Anglo-centric outlook of Ulster's British-based trade unionism, and the need for northern policy to be run from Belfast.

> Unionism is still the strongest political force in Ulster but it is being steadily broken up by labour. Hibernianism is still strong but also weakening. Republicanism is weak and, comparatively speaking, is not advancing, while Liberalism is now a negligible quantity.
>
> Labour, which for lack of guidance retains an English outlook, is the only political force which is making any headway towards breaking up the reaction attitude of the Ulster people. Helped of course by the general unrest, it had succeeded in creating a much less conservative atmosphere. If left to itself, however, labour in Ulster, both Catholic and non-Catholic would again harden the mental attitude of the North East into another type of anti-Irish and pro-English attitude. The time is therefore ripe to take hold of the now fluid state of mind in Ulster and to mould it to a national outlook.
>
> The paper 'The Northern Democrat' was founded by the writer and it was an attempt to produce such an effect. For this purpose it was put in the hands of Belfast Labour men, but, as may be seen from the files, these men left to themselves would have an anglicizing rather than a nationalising effect. The experiment was valuable in that it showed us clearly the proper method of dealing with the situation. It brought to light the danger of allowing Ulster Labour to develop along its own lines and it also showed that a section of the labour men led by Councillor James Baird were definitely groping their way towards an Irish national position.
>
> It showed that any paper placed in the hands of Labour in Ulster would gravitate to the strongest section, which is based on English traditions of Labour, and that our policy ought to be, to run such a paper ourselves with a view towards...strengthening the hands of those labour men of Irish sympathies.[30]

Patterson wanted Sinn Féin to launch a new *Northern Democrat*, based on the Democratic Programme, to 'educate and organise the attitude of Irish Labour in centres of English industry especially that of North East Ulster', and run by a Belfast group centred on Joe Connolly. He claimed that the scheme was 'strongly endorsed' by Connolly and Eoin MacNeill. Connolly, from west Belfast, had served on the Dáil Commission of Inquiry into the Resources and Industries of Ireland. MacNeill, MP for Derry City, was Dáil Minister for Industry. Patterson estimated that it would cost £64 per week to produce an eight-page paper with a print run of 5,000, and a full-time editor, circulation manager, and two circulation agents.

Dáil Éireann's cabinet discussed the proposition at two meetings and passed it over to MacNeill. MacNeill spoke on 'Ireland's future, a co-operative commonwealth' to the Derry Workers' Education Committee at a sizable meeting in the Guildhall in September. The committee had been set up by Peadar O'Donnell as a nucleus of a branch of the James Connolly College in Dublin, and MacNeill's was to be the first talk in a series.[31] That same month, Patterson published the monthly *Red Hand Magazine* to advance his perspective. The *Red Hand Magazine* featured a few gestures to socialism and ran to four issues, folding in December. It marked the end of Patterson's project. Unfortunately for Patterson, loyalists were already thinking along the same lines from the other end of the spectrum, and had struck first, shattering hopes of unity through socialism, in July. Oddly, given its lean towards Protestants and concern to be realistic, *Red Hand* did not address the workplace expulsions.

Meanwhile, Baird's rising profile was evident on May Day. After an absence of some years, the tradition of marking international workers' day was revived in Belfast in 1919 with a huge procession. Legend puts the turnout at 100,000. Steady rain and cold wind meant the following year's festivities did not draw the same crowds. It was an impressive occasion nonetheless and, fortuitously, a Saturday. Trade union contingents led off from Donegall Place at 3.30pm escorted by several bands. A noted presence was two brakes carrying children from the socialist Sunday school. The route took them to Ormeau Park and a demonstration under the auspices of the Belfast Labour Party. Baird was on the first of three platforms, and seconded the main resolution, a lengthy pledge of solidarity with the peoples of the defeated Central Powers and with the Russian people in 'their new-found power'. It also 'protest[ed] strongly against the use of black troops on the Continent as in our opinion it will lead to worse trouble than already exists'. There had been widespread objections in Germany and elsewhere to the deployment of colonial soldiers in the French army of occupation. A front-page article in British Labour's *Daily Herald* on 10 April was headed 'Black scourge in Europe. Sexual horror let loose by France on the Rhine'. The author was E. D. Morel, who had exposed Belgian savagery in the Congo, and yet remained convinced of the superior intellect of the white race. The Irish section of the Women's International also supported Morel. No mention was made of Morel's call for Dominion self-government for all of Ireland, with special safeguards for Ulster. The Belfast resolution concluded with demands for control of rents, bread, milk, and coal, municipal restaurants, a 44-hour week, and better treatment of ex-servicemen. Baird spoke on the international situation, and urged the resumption of normal trade between Britain and Soviet Russia and 'the Republic of Germany'. Implying that he had a hand in drafting the resolution, he said he made no apology for the inclusion of a reference to Russia.[32]

While the BTUC and Labour Party May Day assemblies in London's Hyde Park called for the withdrawal of the British army from Ireland and for Irish self-determination, the Belfast resolution, and most speeches, studiously ignored Irish events. The one exception was Samuel Porter. Amidst cries of dissent, Porter denounced the Government of Ireland Act, capturing the essence of northern Labour anti-partitionism he went on:

> It was born in bigotry – religious bigotry of the worst kind – and was brought forth in iniquity. It was skilfully designed for the purpose of giving a perpetual power of domination to a small clique of Orange capitalists, who thought that when they got their six-county Parliament they could rule the workers with a rod of iron and make this part of the country a veritable paradise for profiteers. A further objection to the Bill was that it would sever Irish labour in twain: it would cut the North from the South.[33]

The *News-Letter* was astonished by the 'Barrister's outburst'.

Baird had an excellent record of attendance at council and committee meetings up to July 1920.[34] On housing especially, he became increasingly vocal. In May he moved that the Corporation freeze rents on shop, offices, and housing until supply exceeded demand, and in June he warned councillors that if they delayed the construction of new housing, people might 'take possession of existing houses. They would not consent to have three or four families living in a little hovel when a mile or so away there was a mansion with only three or four occupants'. The Unionists were becoming more than irritated by Baird. 'Is it not time that this man ceased preaching anarchy? ,' demanded one councillor, 'If I were Lord Mayor I would settle you soon'.[35] The settlement came soon enough.

CHAPTER 4

Belfast Confetti

We all waited...to see what action would be taken by the Trade Unions, whose rules have been defied, and whose very existence threatened by the authors of the Belfast outbreak. But now it appears that...the Trade Unions can do very little...
Joseph MacRory, Catholic Bishop of Down and Connor.[1]

Half the trouble over the Belfast expulsions arises through certain of the British unions being anxious above all else to retain their Ulster members. This is not trade unionism but one-eyed officialism.
The *Communist*, 26 November 1921.

On 21 July 1920, the first full day of production after the 12th holiday, notices were posted, ostensibly by the Belfast Protestant Association, in the shipyards and on approach roads calling all 'Protestant and Unionist' workers to attend a dinner-hour meeting at the gates of Workman, Clark's south yard. Workman, Clark was regarded as the more stridently Orange of the two shipbuilding companies. Estimates of the number present varied from 2–5,000. The main topic was the Irish Republican Army (IRA) war in 'the south and west', notably the assassination of RIC Commander Gerald Smyth in Cork on 17 July. Smyth was a native of Banbridge. It was also said that Catholics from 'the south and west' had taken the jobs of Protestants who had enlisted during the First World War, and were now keeping loyal ex-servicemen unemployed. Men of the Ulster Ex-Servicemen's Association were present to emphasise the point. The British government was criticised for not accepting Sir Edward Carson's offer to organise Protestants to assist the army and RIC. The recent rioting in Derry was seen as an example of Sinn Féin penetration of Ulster. There was infiltration too of the trade unions, who were no longer representing Protestant interests according to two speakers from the Ulster Workers' Union. Socialists and Sinn Féiners were depicted as the twin enemies of the Protestant working class. A resolution was adopted that all workers should sign a declaration of opposition to Sinn Féin. By 3.30pm, some 300–1,000, mainly apprentices and rivet boys from Workman, Clark's yard and engine works, were marching through Harland and Wolff swinging sledgehammers and ordering out Catholics and Protestants who were identified with socialism.[2] The expulsions would alter the course of James Baird's life and change forever his relationship with Belfast.

Socialist apologists for Unionism like to problematise the tragedy, noting, for example, the rise in unemployment in the spring of 1920. There were about 27,000 employed by the two shipyards, some 2,000 less than in 1919.[3] But to assume that workers were anticipating a slump is to be wise after the event. Insecurity was chronic for yardmen, who were accustomed to volatility and economic cycles. The July 1920 report of the Boilermakers' Belfast District Committee noted high unemployment in the trade while all local berths had vessels on the stocks and attributed the paradox to disruption in the supply of steel from Britain. It had been assured by employers that the difficulties were temporary and the yards would soon be back 'in full swing'. Meanwhile, it was happy to 'wait and see and hope'.[4]

If it was to save Protestant jobs, it was a singular action and extraordinarily coincidental in timing. The death of Smyth may be treated in a similar vein. 'Whataboutery' is an old game in Ulster. The reasons for the expulsions are plain. The evictors gave three: Britain's failure to stop the IRA, Sinn Féin infiltration of Labour, and the desire to recover jobs taken by Catholics during the war. Similar stories about Catholics grabbing Protestant jobs were being retailed in Derry.[5] The diversity of the excuses is suspicious. When three separate vindications are offered for something, there's usually a fourth explanation. The *Belfast News-Letter* of 22 July could think of no justification for the savagery other than the unlikely scenario of a 'Sinn Féiner' shouting 'Up the rebels' at the dinner-hour meeting. Tut-tutting the response, it advised the loyalists to pursue their righteous indignation about the IRA through management. That afternoon's *Belfast Telegraph* could find no one trigger for the outbreak. But there's an underlying convergence to the explanations: they were all reasons to eject Catholics and rotten Prods. Shipyardmen had a tradition of using Catholics as political hostages. All of the Home Rule crises – one could call the run-up to the Government of Ireland Act the fourth Home Rule crisis – led to expulsions. At the same time, each round of expulsions had its unique features. Events in 1920 featured an unprecedented level of collusion by the Unionist leadership, and were distinctive in their emphasis on combatting socialism. In the post-war years, loyalist anti-labourism reflected a wider, European anxiety about the march of Bolshevism. When the evictions escalated into a pogrom, the civil strife commanded an unusual level of backing from the Unionist middle class. As a skilled worker, a Protestant, and a socialist politician who would end up embracing republicanism, Baird became emblematic of the peculiarities of Belfast in 1920.

More complex is the question of who planned the expulsions and to what end? Reaction had been seething for months among Unionists who protested their Labour credentials. Labour Unionism remained attractive to Tory working men, and was finding its feet as a voice of what it termed bona fide trade unionists in opposition to 'Bolshevik and Sinn Féin Labour'. The world war produced a web of overlapping 'patriotic' workers' organisations in the UK, in which Unionist leaders had a prominent role. In late January 1920 the UULA drew sizable attendances to meetings for three MPs from the National Democratic and Labour Party, which emerged from the British Workers' League, a pro-war and pro-imperial splinter from the British Socialist Party and the Labour Party. The three UULA MPs associated with the National Democratic Party at Westminster, and the visiting MPs served as a riposte to a British Labour Party deputation's presence in Dublin.[6] The UULA also had an industrial wing in the Ulster Workers' Union, led by UULA vice-president James Turkington. Further to the right, the British Empire Union, and the Ulster Ex-Servicemen's Association were gaining ground. The Ulster Ex-Servicemen's Association was established in 1919 by Orange members of an early British veterans' fraternity, Comrades of the Great War, who believed, as Orangemen tended to do, that a more loyalist body was more likely to find work for its members. Carson declined to patronise it, deeming it too crass. The Ulster Ex-Servicemen claimed 3,000 members in 1920, and posted certified accounts for the 12 months to November 1921 showing an income from subscriptions and donations of £457.[7] A more shadowy formation is likely to have triggered the expulsions directly: the Belfast Protestant Association/ Ulster Protestant Association. The former had been operational in the shipyards since the 1890s but had faded with the growing militancy of mainstream Unionism after the 1906 general election. Whether it was revamped in 1920 or had its name used as a cover by the UULA is unclear. Its nebulous character is underpinned by the fact that it was also referred to as the Ulster Protestant Association. The Ulster Protestant Association caught the RIC's attention in the autumn of 1920, when it was described as an organisation of 'well-disposed citizens': 'well-disposed' was RIC speak for loyalists friendly towards the authorities.[8] Given its trusted role in the vigilance committees, it may have established its credentials in the shipyards prior to the expulsions. Before long, the RIC were designating it a violent gang of assassins. Unionist leaders continued to use it as a proxy up to its suppression in 1923.[9]

The emergence of these organisations made the 1920 expulsions more organised, articulate, brazen, and lasting in impact than those of the earlier Home Rule crises. The Ulster Protestant Association was instrumental in the formation of the vetting and vigilance committees that would replace shop stewards in the shipyards. From press reports, Morgan identifies 14 leaders of the aggression. Eight worked in Harland and Wolff, and at least four were in Workman, Clark. All were skilled or semi-skilled. Most were plater's helpers, a grade organised by the NAUL, but working as assistants to boilermakers. Among the others were a joiner, a riveter, and an electrician's helper. Just one had been an active trade unionist, in the Boilermakers' Society. Three were in the UULA. The men who carried out the expulsions were likely to be young and unskilled or semi-skilled, plater's helpers again being numerous.[10] There is no record of anyone trying to stop them. The *Belfast Telegraph* reported 'no cessation of labour in any department' and the men knocking off as usual.[11]

COMBUSTION OR CONSPIRACY?

If not due to spontaneous indignation, there must have been planning behind the expulsions, though the evidence is circumstantial. Labour successes in the 1920 local elections especially were seen to weaken the case for six county exclusion. Comments at an election inquest at the West Belfast Unionist Club might be interpreted as prescient or a self-fulfilling prophesy:

> until the employers of Belfast took up their proper position and ceased employing Sinn Féiners and other rebels from the South and West they could never hope to occupy their right [sic] position in the city which had been built up by Protestant energy and enterprise. The murders going on throughout the country might before long lead to retaliations.[12]

Patterson, a passionate opponent of theses that Unionism manipulated the working class, acknowledged that the UULA was intent on 'purifying' labour and that the 'thoroughness [and] militancy' of the expulsions was due to the UULA.[13] The UULA minutes say nothing on the expulsions – itself somewhat suspicious – but log appeals to Carson for a volunteer force and urge a big turnout for Belfast Corporation's special session on the expulsions.[14]

The pro-Liberal *Westminster Gazette* of 24 July ridiculed Sir Hamar Greenwood, the last Chief Secretary for Ireland, who joined the dots between the assassination of Smyth and the 'outbursts' in Belfast.

> It is common knowledge in Belfast, and has been frequently admitted by individual Unionists, that plans were matured at least two months ago to

drive all the Home Rule workers in the shipyards out of their employment. The police were well aware of the scheme, and the question discussed by them was not would the attack come but when it would do so.

The *Gazette* noted that the RIC divisional commander in Belfast, Sir William Hacket Pain, had been chief of staff to the commandant of the Ulster Volunteers in 1912. In 1922 he became Unionist MP for South Londonderry. Carson's speech to an assembly of 25,000 at the premier Orange 'field' at Finaghy on 12 July 1921 is much quoted for its astonishing candour:

> We know well that the real battlefield of Ireland in relation to a Republic will be in Ulster. (Cheers)...And, mind you, they have all kinds of insidious methods and organizations at work. Sometimes it is the Church. That does not make much way in Ulster. The more insidious method is tacking on the Sinn Féin question and the Irish Republican question to the Labour question. (A voice – 'Ireland is the most Labour centre in the United Kingdom'). I know that. What I say is this – these men who come forward posing as friends of Labour care no more about Labour than does the man in the moon. Their real object and the real insidious nature of their propaganda is that they may mislead and bring about disunity amongst our own people...[15]

'And these are not mere words,' he added, 'I am sick of words without action'. Less well-known is that the speech followed lobbies to Carson from the UULA and Ulster Ex-Servicemen's Association. Unionist leaders were already pressing the government for the creation of a special constabulary based on the Ulster Volunteer Force. Disturbances would make their case. Morgan notes that Carson 'did not push the connection with Smyth too far, and showed a concern to have "the best men of the labouring classes" enrolled in the police'.[16] Letters echoing the points made by Carson appeared in the *Belfast News-Letter* on 16 July. Rumours materialised and some Catholics got friendly warnings of trouble ahead. The *Irish Times* detected house swapping with Catholics and Protestants trading residences in good humour on the streets.[17]

The purge of the shipyards was ruthless. 'A number were flung into the river', wrote Baird, 'and while struggling for life were pelted with rivets and washers' – the notorious 'Belfast confetti' – 'others were brutally beaten, but the majority, learning of the fate of their fellows, escaped injury by beating a hasty retreat, leaving behind costly tools and other personal belongings'.[18] By late afternoon, all Catholics had left the yard. That evening trams carrying shipyardmen were attacked in the Markets and North Street and spirit groceries and pubs in Ballymacarrett were looted. The liquor trade was associated with Catholics, and spirit groceries, usually located on side streets, were despised as the cheap and insidious end of the market. The local rector, Revd John Redmond, mustered a vigilante corps and the Lord Mayor quickly had them enrolled as special constables. In the shipyards, vigilance committees developed from 28 July to ensure that expellees did not return to work, and later came together as a joint vigilance committee.[19]

Next day the terror spread to factories and mills. No more than a quarter of victims were from the shipyards – Patterson put the number of victimised yardmen at 2,250 – though some expulsions were initiated by apprentices and rivet boys from the yards who toured large works like Sirocco engineering.[20] By the end of the week, 5,000 had lost their jobs and violence, burning and looting had extended to working class areas in east and north Belfast.[21] The victimisation went well beyond the industrial centres and included dockers and hotel workers, and sectors like railwaymen who had formerly maintained unity in the face of severe political pressure.[22] An undated Dáil paper gave the following breakdown:

4.1 *Approximate number of workers expelled in Belfast*

Occupation/union/gender	number	Occupation/union	number
Fitters	300	Shipwrights	40
Joiners	400	Painters	26
Moulders	80	Smiths and strikers	35
Machinists	90	Sawyers	6
Electricians	85	Upholsterers	12
Cabinet and pattern makers	30	French polishers	12
Boilermakers	50	Crane drivers	16
Brassfinishers	40	Workers' Union	800
Iron turners	60	NAUL	500
Coppersmiths	16	Seamen and firemen	120
Hacklesetters	20	Transport workers and dockers	100
Sheet metal workers	12	Non-union	2,000
Women	1,800	Miscellaneous	700

(Source: NA, Dáil Éireann papers, 'Belfast: atrocities on Catholics, 1920-21', DE 2/353).

By October, the Expelled Workers' Relief Committee (EWRC) had registered 8,140 as forced out of their jobs. About one quarter were

Protestants, 2,000 were women, 1,000 were Catholic ex-servicemen, and less than 1,400 were skilled. At least half were heads of families.[23] The true figure is impossible to calculate as others deemed it wise to leave of their own volition, affected by what would now be called 'the chill factor'. Some reports put the numbers victimised and evicted at 20,000. In October Baird estimated that there were 10,000 affected directly by the pogrom, and that their dependents amounted to a further 30,000. The same figures were later cited by the American Committee for Relief in Ireland (Amcomri), set up in the wake of the Burning of Cork in December 1920. The White Cross, established in February 1921 to assist with the disbursal of Amcomri funds, put the total number affected by the Belfast workplace expulsions at 20,000.[24]

Dáil Éireann recorded the burning of four houses in Baird's former street, Beersbridge Road, in July, and a further 71 elsewhere in Belfast. A second wave of violence began on 24 August. Three calls to the fire-brigade were made from Beersbridge Road on the evening of 26th. Thirty-six Catholic homes in Ballymacarrett had been burned by the end of the day. By October, the Revd Redmond reckoned that 209 pubs or spirit groceries had been wrecked, 58 of them in Ballymacarrett. Seizing the opportunity to advance temperance, Protestant clerics then orchestrated a campaign to stop the re-opening of Ballymacarrett's spirit groceries. All Catholic owned businesses were vulnerable, and the targets included draperies, jewellers, news agents, butchers, barbers, bootmakers, and fruiterers. Another casualty was the North Belfast ILP hall in Langley Street, razed to the ground by loyalists. The foundation stone had been laid by Keir Hardie in 1910.[25] What the White Cross described as a 'peculiarly savage outburst' erupted in July 1921 when 161 houses in the Lower Falls were destroyed. Some were re-housed in a new street called Amcomri Street.[26] The existence of armed Hibernians, the National Volunteers, and the IRA in Belfast ensured that the pogrom turned into civil strife. Communal troubles in the city would last for two years, and result in the deaths of 267 Catholics and 185 Protestants. Over 2,000 were wounded.[27] The nationalist explanation of events was reflected in the conclusion of the American Commission on Conditions in Ireland: 'the Ulster pogroms were not primarily due to a spontaneous flare-up of smoldering bigotry, but were rather promoted by those whose economic and political interests were opposed both to strong labour [trade] unionism and to Irish republicanism'.[28] From the United States, Éamon de Valera expressed incredulity that Belfast workers would play the game of 'exploiting British capitalists who are endeavouring to put the workers at each others' throats'.[29]

From the outset it was evident that Labour bodies in Belfast would pursue differing responses, depending on how much, or how little, they wanted to confront loyalists. The first attempt to organise expelled workers was frustrated by the military, who banned a meeting called for Monday, 26 July. Another was then allowed to be held on the Wednesday in St Mary's Hall, officially St Mary's Catholic Hall, in central Belfast, where the curate was Fr John Hassan. Hassan began sending reports to Dublin and his despatches would form the basis of his *Facts and Figures of the Belfast Pogroms* under the pseudonym G. B. Kenna. The meeting had set up the EWRC, which would be led by Baird and John Hanna. John Alexander Hanna, no relation to the Labour Unionist of that name, hailed from Jerusalem Street in south Belfast's Holyland, then a Protestant district of artisan dwellings near Queen's University. Like his father, and like Baird, he worked as a boilermaker in Harland and Wolff and was a Presbyterian, but at 22 years old he was much younger. He had stood as an Independent Labour candidate in Cromac in the 1920 municipal elections, polling a mere 57 first preferences. In the wake of the expulsions he described himself as 'a loyalist – a loyalist to my class' – and 'a Labour man first and an Irish Nationalist afterward'.[30]

The EWRC's address would be St Mary's Hall and it claimed to represent 90% of expelled workers. The district committee of the ASCJ also set up a relief committee, based in the Artizans' Hall in Garfield Street. Four hundred of the 1,390 expelled skilled workers were joiners. They were the biggest single group of expelled men, and included the ASCJ's executive member for Ireland. In June, joiners at Workman, Clark had voted to dissociate themselves from their executive's support for 'the aspirations of Sinn Fein'.[31] A third committee was set up by the Amalgamated Engineering Union (or AEU as the ASE had become since 1 July) in Clonard Street Hall, off the Falls Road. The union paid lockout rather than victimisation pay to its 300 expelled fitters on the ground that the expulsions were 'retaliatory'. James Freeland, its Belfast district secretary, said little on the expulsions in his monthly reports. Simon Greenspon encountered a similar response in the Electrical Trades Union, where the executive referred him to the British Labour Party. John Milan, District Organiser of the union and a comrade of Greenspon in the Belfast Labour Party, supplied Harland and Wolff with the names of replacements for the expelled sparks, and insisted that negotiations to resolve the problem include the vigilance committees. The Belfast lodge of the United Operative Plumbers and Domestic Engineers was already under loyalist control and opposed the union executive's attempts to set up a lockout fund. Efforts by the FEST to set up a joint committee were frustrated by the UULA.[32] In the National Union of Railwaymen, the executive committee condemned the victimisation of Catholic railwaymen and established a subscription fund, but some members wrote to the *Railway Review* defending the expulsions and deploring 'a fund which would be used for the disruption of the British Empire'.[33] The Irish Nationalist Veterans' Association opened a register for expelled ex-servicemen, who numbered about 700.[34]

The Boilermakers' Society was ambivalent. In politics, the leadership had endorsed the British Labour Party's call for the withdrawal of troops from Ireland and Russia, self-determination for Ireland, an embargo on trade unionists handling munitions of war for Ireland or Russia, and backed strike action to enforce those demands if necessary.[35] Where its trade union interests were concerned, it was a different matter. John Hill, general secretary of the Boilermakers, initially deplored the denial of work to those who 'profess the Southern political faith' and set up a relief fund. Months later, as part of a BTUC fact-finding mission to Belfast, Hill would whitewash the loyalists. The annual report of the Boilermakers' Belfast District Committee made its own excuses, contradicting those citing unemployment as a cause of the expulsions:

> During the first six months of the year our local shipbuilding was held up for want of material, but towards mid-summer the import of steel improved and delivery became more regular, so that our hopes were centred on more regular employment after the July holidays; but events proved our hopes were not to be realised just then, as Sinn Féiners were on the warpath in the neighbourhood of Belfast. The murder of District Inspector Swanzy on Sunday, 22 July, brought about that political strife which we all deplore. That base and cowardly murder so inflamed the passion of the people that the desire for retaliation took possession of them, who, up to that date, were living together in peace and harmony.[36]

Baird responded with a letter in the Boilermakers' *Monthly Review* in March pointing out that Swanzy had been killed on 22 August and comparing the District Committee with the Biblical liar Ananias. The real cause of the disturbances, he said, was economic. Dividing the workers through sectarianism was the employers' reaction to the growing power of labour.

With trade unions so at odds and so timorous, employers found it tempting to hit the ball back into their court. Hanna recalled:

> We sent a deputation to the management of Harland and Wolff's to see if the men affected could be segregated in order that we may have a sporting chance and to have a military guard placed at the entrance to the place where we would be working. That was turned down. We suggested to the management to close down the works and give the Orangeman a dose of his own physic and teach him the hardships of unemployment. They told us that

the hooligan element would break loose and that property would suffer. So you see that property in Belfast, as in other towns, is more sacred than life.[37]

Representatives of the ASCJ were told as much. Hanna declined a management offer of redeployment to Birmingham. After making a vague promise to restore normality, Lord Pirrie, the chairman of Harland and Wolff, temporised. In mid August, he told a deputation from the Scottish Trades Union Congress that while men of all religions had the right to employment, the crux lay in Protestant insistence on declarations of loyalty, which Catholics were refusing to sign. The declarations of loyalty were a key defence against the charge of sectarianism.[38] Just as loyalists said their objection was to men from 'the south and west' rather than local Catholics, so too did they insist their animus was political rather than religious. In September Harland's wrote to unions suggesting a conference at which all parties could set out their views, but that too came to nothing.[39]

Neither would the authorities help. On 26 July Baird and Davy Campbell had requested a special session of the Corporation to discuss the reinstatement of expellees and the appointment of cross-community peace patrols.[40] Ominously, their sole support came from three Sinn Féin councillors, and it prompted a loyalist rally at Harland and Wolff during the dinner-hour on Friday 30th and protests about Labour deserting workers for Sinn Féin. To calm the passions, Baird and Campbell immediately wrote to the Lord Mayor withdrawing their request. Campbell followed up with a telephone call to His Worship at 2am on Saturday and was of the opinion that the special sitting would be cancelled. He and Baird did not attend. Setting the tone, a deputation of 15 loyalist shipyardmen, mostly plater's helpers 'clad in their dongaree suits', was received by the Corporation to warn they 'would not be responsible for any consequences' should the resolution be passed. With 'lively' yardmen festooning one of the public galleries with Union Jacks, waving revolvers, filling the air with tobacco smoke and 'coarse language', and throwing missiles, it was left to four Sinn Féin councillors – one left early – and one Nationalist to brave the toxic climate and propose the Corporation act to restore evicted families to their homes and expelled workers to their jobs. The motion was defeated 35-5 in favour of an amendment that the government take 'stern measures' against the 'assassins' who 'have awakened universal indignation in the entire Loyalist population'.[41] Unionist councillors and the gallery broke into 'God Save the King'. The Unionist press taunted the Labour men for their absence, and the *Northern Whig* sneered at 'the Labour socialists who ran away'. An unseemly wrangle ensued. Baird protested that the Lord Mayor had agreed to cancel the meeting, but His Worship denied it. When Baird claimed that he and Campbell had been out of Belfast, it was alleged that they had both been spotted in Royal Avenue that morning. When Baird said they had arrived in the city centre after the meeting, the sighting was put, precisely, at 'two minutes past eleven', the hour the session opened.[42]

A fund to help expellees was set up in mid-August, and an appeal issued, which represented the expulsions as an attack on Labour in language which drew on Christianity and socialism.

> It was conceived and prepared months ago. It did not originate amongst the workers themselves. Certain workers, whose religious and political rancour made them ready instruments, were secretly instigated to stir up the flames of sectarian bitterness.
> But the wire-pulling and the secret instigation were the work of a political and Capitalistic caucus, who sought to break up the ranks of Labour. Their plan was the old one – 'Divide and Conquer'...
> The only way to meet this is to arraign the wrong-doers at the bar of Public Opinion, and to frustrate this manoeuvre of selfish Capitalism by economic action. Such action must be prompt and thorough...
> We appeal for means to help these workers in their trouble, but we appeal also to the Industrial World for Industrial Justice.
> Everyone has a Right to Live by his Wages. If this Right is lost, all is lost. If religious bigotry or political rancour, engineered by selfish and insidious Capitalists, is allowed to imperil this God-Given Right, then the position of Labour will be undermined.[43]

The appeal was signed by Fr P. Convery, parish priest, P. Finnegan and John Doherty, both from the St Vincent de Paul, and six Labour men: Joseph Fegan, secretary, expelled workers' committee, ASCJ, Joseph T. Clark, expelled workers' committee, Electrical Trades Union, Daniel McRandall, district secretary, ASCJ, Alexander Stewart, vice-president, Belfast trades council, W. H. Carruthers, secretary, Belfast Labour Party, and Baird, who was described as a councillor and member of the Belfast Labour Party. The fund's treasurer, Fr Convery, had been treasurer of the expelled workers' committee in 1912.[44] Most of the assistance given the expelled workers came from local Catholic agencies, Sinn Féin sources, and, from 1921, the White Cross. Bishop MacRory and Joe Devlin, Nationalist MP for Belfast West, were quick to set examples. In Britain, the EWRC operated through the Labour movement and Irish organisations like the United Irish League, the Ancient Order of Hibernians, and the Irish Self-Determination League. The EWRC also lobbied in the United States, Canada, Australia, France, Spain, and Belgium.[45] The ITGWU sent Councillor Denis Houston to Scotland, where numerous expellees had gone in search of employment. Houston assisted with cross-channel relief work and fundraising for several weeks.[46] St Mary's Hall became a hub of activity. A delegation from the BTUC in December was impressed:

We visited St. Mary's Hall, which is the centre from which relief funds are being distributed, where every opportunity was offered us of obtaining information. The arrangements were very well organised, and altogether 9,000 unemployed people were on the books. The amount of assistance allowed was £1 per week to married men and 10s. to single men or unemployed women. There was a fair percentage of unemployed women workers owing to slack conditions in the linen mills and a good many who had been indirectly affected by the disturbance in July. To the foregoing allowance had to be added the State Unemployment Benefit and any benefit the worker might receive from his union; the total in the best of cases would fall materially short of what even an unskilled workman might receive in the shipyards. The majority of the recipients were unskilled, but a substantial number were skilled workmen.[47]

For 'action', the EWRC turned initially to the Irish and British congresses. The ITUC, meeting in Cork, suspended standing orders to hear Hanna, Travers, and O'Donoghue from the EWRC on 4 August. Travers opened his remarks in Irish. All three stressed that the victims were both Catholic and Protestant, and that the real target was organised labour. 'At first sight', said Travers,

this matter may seem a mere recurrence of Orange bigotry, and but simply and solely a religious question. It is not. It is first, last and all the time an economic question. The capitalists view with alarm the progressive spirit that is sweeping over this country. They see that Sinn Fein, the Republican element, is breaking the old political prejudices and barriers; and that the Labour movement equally is broadening the Orangeman's mind so quickly that it would be only a matter of time when the Boyne would be bridged, and that then the ascendancy gang would lose their power.[48]

The Congress condemned the expulsions with acclamation and instructed the national executive to take 'immediately whatever action they may deem necessary to protect the interests of our fell-workers' but left it to the executive to decide what that meant and rejected a call to levy affiliates. The executive sent its secretary, Tom Johnson, and J. T. O'Farrell of the British-based Railway Clerks' Association, to Belfast and donated £50 to the EWRC for fund-raising and propaganda in Britain. Arguing that the key lay with the unions concerned, the ITUC did nothing else.[49]

That year's BTUC annual conference opened in Portsmouth on 6 September. There were just three delegates from Belfast, a shipwright and two members of the Workers' Union, and none of them spoke on the expulsions. The Standing Orders Committee received a deputation of expellees, and agreed to submit their emergency resolution instructing the parliamentary committee to convene the executives of the unions affected, with a view to taking 'a common line of action' to get the expelled men reinstated. The Congress president set the context: 'You will be aware that in the anxiety to uphold the Union Jack in Belfast men are being prevented from working because of their political and religious opinions'. John Beard, president of the Workers' Union, which had 800 members expelled, seconded, and was more candid: 'The less said about this matter the better...It is no use discussing the merits or demerits of the particular question – both sides had prevented each other from working, and we have this regrettable state of affairs upon which we should try to get agreement'. Beard was contradicted by the final speaker on the motion, F. Lowe, Manchester, who delivered a powerful description of events from a recent visit to victimised members of his own union, the House and Ship Painters. Dismissing the idea that the trouble was 'some religious controversy', he reviewed too the inadequacy of seeing it in terms of orange and green, and got to the kernel: 'the peculiar thing has been that every man who took an active part in the Trade Union movement and the Labour movement in Belfast has been absolutely driven from the island, and for no other crime than that committed at the ballot box in the last municipal election'. As the vote was about to be carried a Sunderland shipwright protested that the matter should be left entirely to Belfast, and 'amid some excitement proceeded to invite the Congress...to consider well about it'.[50] Lowe had personal cause for consideration on his next visit to Belfast. His remarks at Portsmouth landed him in hot water, and he found a note in his hotel room from 'The Ulster Division', complete with skull and crossbones, giving him five hours to leave town.[51] The parliamentary committee agreed to send a troika to Belfast consisting of Hill, A.A. Purcell, and Arthur Pugh. Alf Purcell had been treasurer of the FEST and supervised the Irish branches of the National Amalgamated Furnishing Trades Association. Pugh was general secretary of the Iron and Steel Trades Confederation. All were regarded as being among the BTUC's 'lefts'[52] Like many British 'lefts', they sympathised with Irish self-determination except when applied to trade union organisation.

Similarly, and mindful that the Irish in Britain largely voted Labour, the British Labour Party gradually shifted its position on Ireland from Home Rule to self-determination and appointed a commission of enquiry. In November and December 1920, Johnson guided a British Labour Party delegation around scenes of crown forces' atrocities in Dublin and Munster to compile an indictment of British government policy. The fact-finding tour led the Ulster Unionist Council to counter with a booklet *The Labour Party and Ireland*. In respect of the expulsions at least, the Unionists had nothing to worry about. The commission did not visit Ulster, its report said nothing on the north, and the EWRC failed to persuade the British Labour Party to back the Belfast Boycott. As the party expressed its concern to remain in step with the Irish Labour Party, the ITUC has to bear some responsibility. The difference in approach to Ireland between the two wings of the British Labour movement was stark. On 29 December, the British Labour Party convened a special conference of 800 delegates in London's Central Hall. Johnson addressed the delegates and, always eager to avoid conflict, did not mention Belfast.[53] More than 500 Labour meetings on Ireland followed in January and February 1921. Each called on the Parliamentary Labour Party to demand a judicial enquiry into reprisals, and to promote negotiations with Sinn Féin and the withdrawal of troops. The Labour commission's report stressed that 'as the Irish people have faith in British Labour alone among the political parties' in Britain, Labour should be central to a peace settlement.[54] Party chairman Arthur Henderson made another appeal for peace in the pamphlet *Nonconformity and Ireland*, which was published by the Labour Party.[55]

By contrast, the BTUC emphasised that when it came to the expulsions, it was a helpless bystander, and relations between Irish and British trade unions were antagonistic. Meanwhile, serious trouble, more serious in the eyes of the BTUC, had broken out within the ASCJ. British union officials had urged their Belfast committees to work with expelled members, but almost all buckled to a negative response. The ASCJ alone stood firm. Members of its Manchester-based executive visited Harland and Wolff on 24 August and requested the reinstatement and protection of expellees, and an end to religious or political discrimination in the shipyard. They also called a mass meeting of Belfast members for 26 August. Though the venue was to be private, the meeting was proclaimed by the military as likely to cause 'grave disorder'.[56] When it became evident in September that employers would take no action, the ASCJ struck eight companies that refused to facilitate the re-instatement of expelled members: the two shipyards, McLaughlin and Harvey (housebuilders), and Coombe, Barbour, Fairbairn, and Lawson, Musgrave's, Davidson & Company, the Sirocco Works, and Mackie's (all engineering plants). Of about 4,500 affected members, 3,000 ignored the strike call, including seven branch secretaries, and had their union cards withdrawn.[57] Unlike the BTUC, the ASCJ executive was not influenced by pleas that the victimisation had a secular rationale. It insisted to employers on a 'bedrock principle':

> As a Trade Union, we could not tolerate any employer, or Association of Employers, or any workman, or Association of Workmen, imposing on our members conditions on which they would be allowed to earn their livelihood, apart from the conditions laid down in our working rules, and agreed to by the Employers' Association and our own Trade Union organisation in Belfast.

> We could not stand by and permit any faction to divide our membership into what is termed by the rioters, and those who support them, 'loyal' and 'disloyal' workmen…it should not matter whether a man be a Roman Catholic or a Mahommedan, or whether he be a Tory, Liberal, or a Socialist.[58]

Annoyed to see the recalcitrants being 'made much of by the employers', the Society's official history regretted that other unions 'did not see fit to stand with us in our fight for trade union liberty'.[59]

Hill, Purcell, and Pugh finally embarked for Belfast on Saturday 4 December. Guided by the local FEST secretary, they met the FEST and ASCJ district committees, the two shipyard managements, the Assistant Under-Secretary for Ireland, the Lord Mayor of Belfast, the Harbour Commissioners, the Chamber of Commerce, the EWRC, the expelled workers' committee of the AEU, the Joint Vigilance Committee, and an organisation of joiners who supported the expulsions and been expelled in turn from the ASCJ. The vigilantes told them frankly to go home and leave Belfast to settle its own affairs, which they did on 10 December. The troika admitted their presence produced no results other than what they believed to be 'a better feeling among the workmen'.[60] On their return to London, the parliamentary committee convened a meeting of the executives of the unions affected to consider the troika's report. Eighty delegates from 18 unions attended. Two points were clear from the report. First, it regarded the dispute within the ASCJ as being of primary importance, and blamed the executive. Secondly, its view of the expulsions was shaped by the Joint Vigilance Committee. Bizarrely, the section on the 'Causes of the trouble' opened by noting that Belfast was quiet immediately after 12 July, which showed that 'working class solidarity and community of interest are tending to overcome the old sectarian differences'. The troika were willing to make themselves look stupid to obviate Carson's 12 July speech. They then attributed the expulsions to the 'large influx of men from the South and West' to meet the labour shortage during the war, many of them Sinn Féiners it was presumed, and the killing of Smyth. It was understandable, they argued, in the circumstances, that normally law-abiding people would turn vigilante. Concluding the section, the report exonerated employers and stressed their concern to end all religious and political discrimination in their industries. The BTUC now devoted more attention to healing the rift within the Amalgamated Society of Woodworkers, as the ASCJ had become.[61]

The most substantial response to the expulsions was the Belfast Boycott, which formally extended to three other centres of sectarian violence, Lisburn, Dromore, and Banbridge, and was enforced by local committees almost everywhere outside the north-east. The boycott was initiated by Dáil

Éireann on 6 August 1920 on foot of a petition from Sinn Féin councillors and other republicans in Belfast. Though prompted by the expulsions, and administered by the Dáil Department of Labour, it was never exclusively about the workers. The petitioners were concerned too with the pogrom against all 'Sinn Féiners', and the reaction blurred into a broader attempt 'to make Belfast realise that it is in Ireland and must be of Ireland'.[62] There had been talk of an economic embargo to scuttle 'Carsonia' since early 1920, and a spontaneous boycott evolved before coming under Dáil direction. Only Markievicz and Earnán de Blaghd, himself an Antrim Protestant, opposed it in the Dáil. As they feared, it proved to be a blunt instrument, open to sectarian misuse, and had little impact on the culprits, much less on 'the garrison' or 'the pogromists', as northern Unionists were labelled. While it's hard to credit the oft-made claim that it worsened relations with Unionists, it did encourage a vengeful animosity in the south and, ironically, further distanced the south, psychologically, from the benighted north. Belfast's economy was damaged and lost £5million in trade in 1921, but the impact was marginal. Those affected included nationalist owned businesses, which were hit too by a counter-boycott in Belfast.[63] Obtusely, the boycott's director, Joseph McDonagh, TD for Tipperary North and acting Minister for Labour, proclaimed confidently in 1921 that 'Belfast is faced with bankruptcy'.[64]

BAIRD'S ODYSSEY

After the debacle on Belfast Corporation in July 1920, Baird joined the Belfast Labour lobby – Councillor Clarke Scott and Greenspon – in London, which met Labour MPs and Chief Secretary Greenwood. Whatever was said, Greenwood lost his temper and testily told Baird he 'would remember him'. Greenwood had earlier pleaded that he was helpless, telling 'Wee Joe' Devlin that he had 'no power to insist upon employers employing Roman Catholics, Orangemen, or anybody else'.[65] In other respects, the possibilities were more promising. Britain was currently awash with pressure groups on Ireland, such as the Peace With Ireland Council, the Irish Self-Determination League, and the Irish Dominion League, together with campaign committees within the Catholic Church, Liberal Party, the Women's International League, the Union of Democratic Control, and the Labour movement. Against the background of daily press bulletins on the deteriorating condition of Terence MacSwiney, Baird stayed in London during August. According to the nationalist *Ulster Herald*, he and Greenspon addressed 'huge meetings' around the city each day, and received an enthusiastic response.[66] An ad in the *Daily Herald* on 24 August advised: 'Be at Highbury corner, tonight at 8, and hear Comrades

Baird and Greensfor (sic), of the Belfast trades council. Meeting tomorrow outside Finsbury Park Empire'. At one meeting in Hyde Park, addressed by Baird, Greenspon, and Scott, it was found that the law prevented a collection. Baird became a 'cockshot' and £20 was thrown at him. The chairman was arrested and bound over, but the cause remained £20 to the good. London evidently proved sympathetic and the EWRC opened an office at 2 Union Road, N7 in Holloway. It would serve as Baird's London address into 1922.[67] After London, Baird urged an embargo on raw materials to the Belfast shipyards at meetings in Birmingham, Barrow-in Furness, Teesside, Bradford, Leeds, Wales, and the south of Scotland and met with 'financial success'.[68] Feeling that they were losing the propaganda war, the UULA sent three trade unionists in mid-September to speak to 'the loyalists of Liverpool' in Stanley Park. In Belfast, in conjunction with the Unionist Party, it set up a relief fund for Protestants, claiming that many had been driven from their homes and their work, and convened meetings of shipyardmen, urging them to join the Ulster Workers' Union.[69]

In late October Baird visited Dublin, where the Lord Mayor had convened a meeting 'representative of all creeds and classes' to fund the relief of expelled workers on 21 September.[70] Baird hoped

> to get in touch with the well-to-do Protestant portion of the population to put the position in Belfast clearly before them, and to appeal to them as men who have done well and made money in this city, though in a minority, to show in a practical way their disapproval of what is going on in the North.[71]

There were many Protestants in Dublin who could 'well afford a subscription,' he said, adding, 'As a minority, they have been well treated', and were duty-bound to show that the intolerance did not represent them. 'My appeal in the first instance will be to the Protestants of Dublin, meetings of whom, if possible, I shall address, and get into contact with the Protestant clergymen. Very likely I will then proceed all over the South and West...'.[72]

On 7 November he addressed a mass meeting of members of the Irish Engineering, Electric, Shipbuilding, and Foundry Trade Union. This union had been founded in May 1920 as alternative to the British-based craft unions in the electrical and engineering trades. Hill quickly denounced it as politically motivated and an existential threat to the Boilermakers in Ireland, which indeed it was.[73] It had been launched at the prompting of Michael Collins, Constance Markievicz, Minister of Labour, and the 'Labour Board', a cover name for republican agents infiltrating the amalgamateds to push for an exclusively Irish Labour movement. Baird's speech indicated that he too had come to embrace the project. Opening, he said that as an Ulster Protestant it gave him no pleasure to allude to terrible things done in the name of Protestantism. He went on:

> The Irish representatives on the executives of the English unions were Carsonites from Belfast, who acted as their Carsonite masters wished them. As far as trade unionism was concerned, it seemed to him that the sooner they had here one union for workers of hand and brain the better for the workers of Ireland. The religious bogey was stirred up to divide the workers.[74]

However, this was his only reported meeting in Dublin, and a letter to the Dublin *Evening Telegraph* says later suggests that he was still waiting for a response from the city's Protestants.

> **Will the Protestants of Dublin stand forth as one man and denounce this outrage against humanity?**
> Will Protestant clergymen remain silent and allow the world to assume they condone these horrid deeds, or will they with trumpet voice condemn the guilty persons and thus show to all men that Protestantism still stands for civil and religious liberty? [Emphasis in the original].

The letter was published on Armistice Day, which was fast becoming the highpoint of the Dublin Unionist calendar; the only day when one had an excuse to parade the Union Jack in Dublin, but also a day that reminded southern Unionists of their reliance on the goodwill of the nationalist majority. Ignoring Baird, the *Church of Ireland Gazette* presented the violence in Belfast as an attempt by Sinn Féin to extend the war. Its Belfast correspondent repeatedly retailed the loyalist version of events and warned:

> Those Protestants in Dublin and throughout Ireland who are being solicited for subscriptions towards the support of 'expelled' workers in Belfast, should make sure that the money so subscribed will be distributed impartially to Protestants as well as to Roman Catholics who have been obliged to withdraw from their employment. The general impression outside Belfast is that it is only Roman Catholics who are suffering. It is not, apparently, known that hundreds of loyalist families were driven from their homes in Belfast, and are now living in acute distress, owing to the Sinn Féin outrages in the city.[75]

CHAPTER 5

Hellfast

Belfast still Hell-fast: 100 Catholics now homeless: shot
and fire orgy: railmen condemn a foul murder.
Headline, *Daily Herald*, 19 April 1922.

The 19 months after the expulsions were a phase of severe stress for the
Baird family, and saw James involved in two incidents for which he is
best known to historians. In May 1921 he contested the first elections to
the Northern Ireland parliament. It was a gesture both brave and futile,
and reflected a belief, very much in the spirit of James Connolly during
the third Home Rule crisis, that Labour should assert its anti-partition
principles whatever the consequences. The Ulster Hall rally, which was
supposed to launch the Labour campaign, was aborted. The other event
that earned him notoriety was his speech on workplace expulsions to the
BTUC in September. The speech is usually filleted for its confirmation
that the expulsions were directed against 'rotten Prods'. It raised Unionist
animosity against him to new heights, and revived in republican circles
the idea of using people like Baird to advance the national cause in Ulster.
1921 also saw the beginning of Baird's short and controversial career as a
full time union official, and set him on a path that would take him out of
Belfast and ultimately out of Ireland. On returning to Belfast in early 1921,
he had secured a position with the National Sailors' and Firemen's Union
of Great Britain and Ireland (NSFU). Given the union's politics, it was a
curious station, and not one that suited his increasingly forthright anti-
partitionism. From May at least he was making contact with the ITGWU,
and in October he took his entire branch into the ITGWU. From 1922 he
was employed by Liberty Hall as an organiser, and sent to a fresh field of
operations in the south-east.

In February 1921, the Belfast Labour Party decided to consult affiliates about candidates for the upcoming Northern Ireland elections. The voting would be by proportional representation, with the franchise open to men over 21 years and women over 30. In March the party disappointed progressive opinion by announcing that it would not contest. A spokesman explained, disingenuously, that members felt it would be a waste of time as the parliament would not last too long, but individual comrades might go forward. More likely, the party was still reeling from the workplace expulsions and felt uncomfortable about being bracketed with Joe Devlin's appeal for a combined anti-Unionist campaign. Papers like the *Westminster Gazette* were already making that call.[1] Alderman Sam Kyle later wrote that the party was demoralised by defections of those who could not withstand 'the perpetual strain' that came with the 1920 expulsions. Formally, the party's only public activity in May 1921 was to run a sweepstake on the Epsom Derby.[2]

Baird remained in fighting form. He missed all Belfast city council meetings in the three months after July 1920, was present at just two meetings of the council and committees in the last quarter of 1920, missing 29, and did not attend any in 1921 until 1 April. Making up for lost time, he made a noisy intervention as the Lord Mayor moved the minutes, demanding the suspension of standing orders to discuss the Corporation's failure to implement the Provision of School Meals Act. The council was 'an inhuman machine', he shouted, as the Unionists rounded on him.[3]

Expectations of a Labour abstention from elections were confounded on Friday 13 May. Shortly before 11am – nominations closed at noon – Baird, John Hanna, Harry Midgley, and Revd John Bruce Wallace strode into the City Hall with Kyle and other ILP leaders and made their way to the Under-Sheriff's office. Baird, Hanna, and Midgley stood as 'socialists', pledged to boycott the Northern Ireland parliament. 'We are completely against partition,' declared their manifesto, 'It is an unworkable stupidity... the interests of the workers of Ireland are politically and economically one'.[4] Baird's election papers described him as an artizan, residing at 43 Willowholme Street, nominated by Sam Haslett, an ILP'er, and Margaret McCoubrey, Ulster's leading suffragist.[5] Midgley illustrates how extensive anti-partitionism had become on the northern left. Raised in an austere Plymouth Brethren household and influenced by the Brethren's sola scriptura theology and aversion to ritual, Midgley worked in the shipyards as a joiner, and volunteered for the wartime 36th (Ulster) Division, which was recruited largely from the Ulster Volunteer Force. On demobilisation in May 1919, he returned to the shipyards, joined the Belfast Labour Party, and became full-time secretary of the Irish Linenlappers' and Warehouse Workers' Union in 1920. As Northern Ireland consolidated, he moved steadily towards Unionism. Clashes with the clergy during the Spanish Civil War turned him anti-Catholic and he ended his days an Orangeman.[6] Technically, Bruce Wallace stood as an independent. He had retired to the ancestral home in Limavady, where, in 1887, he had dreamed of building a model 'New Harmony' through the Circle Co-operative Company. Wallace had formerly favoured Home Rule and his assentors included Kyle, but he now advocated acceptance of the Government of Ireland Act and ran a separate campaign.[7] A fifth socialist, Alex Adams, stood in County Down. A farmer from Millisle, and a self-styled 'workers' delegate and farmer', Adams took a similar tack to Wallace. Unionists largely ignored Wallace and depicted Adams as a freak candidate for his farming background, who was playing into the hands of Sinn Féin by splitting the Protestant vote in 'the leader's constituency'. Sir James Craig and Éamon de Valera were vying to top the poll in Down. Yet Adams was no joker and would be a linchpin of the Northern Ireland Labour Party in Ards.[8]

Baird, Hanna, and Midgley were backed by ILP stalwarts and covert funding from Sinn Féin, and planned to launch their campaign with a 'Great Labour Meeting' in the Ulster Hall on Tuesday 17 May, for which the Belfast Labour Party paid £20. The party also paid their deposits of £150 each. In the *Irish News* the trio stated, 'We stand for an unpartitioned Ireland based on the goodwill of all who love their native land – north to south and east to west…'. Their advertisements in the *Northern Whig* and the *Belfast News-Letter* were more circumspect and simply urged readers to 'Weigh carefully the merits of the parties and candidates. It is the Poverty, Unemployment, and Insecurity question that matters most to working people'.[9] The circumspection was of no avail. There was speculation that the meeting would be stormy. Loyalists had a sense of ownership of the Ulster Hall and had previously prevented similar meetings taking place there. One of the charges against Baird was that he had voted for the Corporation to allow a Sinn Féin meeting in the hall. Even so, the reaction was unexpected. At a few hour's notice, Robert Boyd, secretary of the Ulster Ex-Servicemen's Association, and Leo Thomas, secretary of the Belfast branch of the British Empire Union, mustered a demonstration. The Ex-Servicemen's Association was especially active in the election campaign. Towards 6pm, led by a brake, a brass band, and a fife and drum 'combination', waving Union Jacks on long poles, with placards reading 'Down with Sinn Féin' and a banner of King William crossing the Boyne, 4,000 men set off in their flat caps and dongarees from the shipyards. Anti-socialist literature was distributed along the way in handbills with captions like 'Is the 'Labour' Party Labour' and 'If we had a Labour government, what would it do?'. As they waited to enter the Ulster Hall, the bands played Orange tunes and there were speeches from the brake emphasising that Baird, Hanna, and Midgley were not subvented by Belfast Labour but connected with the 'Catholic Expelled Workers' Fund'. Midgley subsequently claimed to have toured England collecting money for the expelled workers. The *Northern Whig* headlined its coverage of the event 'True Voice of Belfast Labour'. Anticipating trouble, 200 police stood by and two armoured cars circled the vicinity. Cordial relations were soon established. The bands played God Save the King and the police saluted. A convoy of dusty Crossley tenders trundled by, evidently in from patrolling the countryside. The Islandmen cheered and the Specials laughed and waved back. At 7.15pm, the doors opened and the throng rushed in to plant four big Union Jacks on the platform. The offending trio arrived a little later in a taxi to a torrent of abuse from the yardmen. After chatting with Boyd and Thomas under police protection, they declined an invitation to address the hall on condition they said nothing 'disloyal'. Entering the building via Linenhall Street, they reviewed the options in an ante-room and decided to slip away quietly.[10]

The only speeches of the evening came from loyalists. Alex McKay, a UULA councillor in Bangor, set the tone: 'This is not an Irish question and it is not a religious question; it is a question of Rome becoming the predominant power in the country. We are Protestants; we believe in the faith of Martin Luther.'[11] That all five socialist election candidates were Protestant, or that Midgley was an ex-serviceman, was not allowed to complicate the argument. Baird came in for particular criticism for his advocacy of an embargo on raw materials to Belfast. The platform cabled Craig: 'Mass meeting of loyal shipyard workers who have captured Ulster Hall from Bolsheviks Baird, Midgley, and Hanna request that you address them for a few minutes tonight'. A similar message was sent to Sir Edward Carson. Craig wired back: 'Well done, big and wee yards'. A motion of support for Unionist and UULA candidates in the election was also passed.[12] The trio replied with large ads in the *News-Letter* and the *Whig* on 18 May saying simply 'Civil and Religious Liberty! In Belfast. Vote for Baird, Midgley & Hanna'. They also decided to cancel all further meetings 'owing to official hooliganism'. Other than the distribution of a few handbills condemning partition and 'official Unionism', their campaign was over.[13]

There was still a week to polling day but the prospects were hopeless. The *Irish News* of 18 May carried notices saying 'Labour's Banner, Civil and Religious Liberty, The Ballot is secret. Vote Against Official Hooliganism', and advertising two meetings for Baird, Midgley, and Hanna in Victoria Square and Library Street. Next day the paper announced; 'Labour

Meetings: Owing to Official Hooliganism, We have been compelled to cancel all our meetings'. With the media full of reports about 'outrages' against loyalists in the south and Unionism fighting for its life, Belfast was festooned with bunting, flags, placards, posters, and triumphal arches. On the Shankill Road, residents staged fancy dress parades. A combined meeting of 'nos.2 and 3 branches of the Boilermakers' Society' repudiated 'the claim of Messrs Baird and Hanna to represent Labour, as by their candidature they are only aiding Sinn Féin' and called on all electors to vote Unionist.[14] A pleasantly surprised Unionist press applauded the 'patriotic fervour'. Its principal fear was that the left would split the Protestant vote, reduce the Unionist majority, and render the case for partition less than convincing. There was even pressure on the Plymouth Brethren and Covenanting Presbyterians to drop their anathema on voting as a sinful compromise with the secular world.[15] Printers refused to accept work from Baird, Midgley, and Hanna, and after they and their assentors received threatening letters, they were given police protection on their homes.[16] Polling day passed off quietly, with 'just a few 'scraps'' and gunfire here and there. The results exceeded Unionist expectations. Fleets of cars were busy, queues formed at polling stations, and the turnout topped 90 per cent. In Belfast, all Unionist candidates were elected, taking 15 of the 16 seats in the city. Overall, the Unionists won 40 of the 52 seats in the parliament.[17] The socialists finished at the bottom of the poll and lost their deposits. None had secured more than 1 per cent of the vote. Their poor performance came as a major surprise. 'Belfast notes' in the *Church of Ireland Gazette* credited the Orange Order for doing much to 'preserve Belfast from Bolshevism and other evils of blatant socialism'.[18]

5.1 *Socialist candidates in the Northern Ireland elections, 24 May 1921*

	Official Designation	Constituency	1st Preference Vote
James Baird	Socialist	South Belfast	875
John Hanna	Socialist	West Belfast	367
Harry Midgley	Socialist	East Belfast	645
Revd John Bruce Wallace	Independent	North Belfast	926
Alex Adams	Independent	County Down	1,188

Source: *Belfast News-Letter*, 27 May 1921.

5.2 *The Northern Ireland elections, 24 May 1921, South Belfast*

	Official Designation	1st Preference Vote
Thomas Moles	Unionist	17,948
Hugh MacDowell Pollock	Unionist	5,334
Sir Crawford McCullagh	Unionist	5,068
Dermot Barnes	Sinn Féin	2,719
Mrs Julia McMordie	Unionist	2,372
Bernard McCoy	Nationalist	1,688
James Baird	Socialist	875
Electorate: 40,666 Turnout: 36,566 (90.1%) Quota: 7,261		

Source: *Belfast News-Letter*, 27 May 1921.

In four seat South Belfast Baird faced four Unionists, including one of the two women elected to the first Northern parliament who was paradoxically an opponent of female suffrage. More importantly for his vote, Baird was competing with two nationalists. His transfers from the Unionists were derisory. The *News-Letter* described his campaign as 'a negligible quantity', without saying why. Responding to the Returning Officer, Baird congratulated the four Unionist victors, but complained that he had not been permitted to speak during the campaign: 'the old Puritan morals of the north of Ireland, of which they had been so proud, had departed altogether from Belfast'. Thomas Moles, unapologetic, defended the seizure of the Ulster Hall as a response to Baird's call for an embargo on Belfast and won a round of applause. 'Why,' said Moles, a prominent Churchman, 'didn't he go to his spiritual home in St Mary's Hall if he wanted to hold a meeting?' [19] When Craig wrote to the Lord Mayor asking for the use of the City Hall as a temporary seat for the new parliament, Baird was the only councillor on the Improvement Committee to oppose the request.[20]

STORMY WATERS IN THE NSFU

Baird had become secretary of the Belfast branch of the NSFU at 13 Queen's Square, off Donegall Quay. What form of remuneration he received is unclear. In March 1922 he described himself as a pauper for the past 20 months and living on the dole.[21] Moreover, the NSFU was not a congenial spot for a socialist republican. The union had gone jingo during the World War. The U-boat attacks on merchantmen were given as the reason, but while the NSFU had earned a reputation for militancy during the 'great labour unrest' of 1911–13, it had never been very radical. In

1917 the NSFU attracted widespread condemnation for refusing to carry the British Labour delegates to the proposed socialist peace conference in Stockholm. At its special congress in November 1918, the ITUC voted 99–10 to expel the three NSFU delegates for the union's opposition to the post-war international socialist conference that would convene in Berne in February 1919.[22] The NSFU fielded six candidates in the 1918 general election on a seamen's 'patriot' platform which invoked the King and Carson and called for industrial peace and a ban on the employment of 'enemy aliens'. James H. Bennett, Irish organiser of the NSFU, stood in Pottinger, with a sprinkling of support from right-wing trade union activists, including Jack Beattie, a future socialist republican firebrand. Bennett claimed he had been urged to stand by 'the ladies of the Labour Representation Committee', only to be frustrated by 'the Bolsheviks' of the ILP, who nominated Samuel Porter instead. With Porter a barrister from salubrious Stranmillis, Bennett made much of being 'the only trade union candidate' on the list, whose only alma mater was 'the university of adversity'. Baird had some acquaintance with him. As chairman at the mass meeting of shipyardmen for shorter hours in the Ulster Hall on 5 December, he invited Bennett and other election candidates to speak. Originally from Clontarf, Bennett favoured Home Rule with six county exclusion. He was still damned by the Unionists as 'the Home Ruler from Dublin'. Porter was vehemently anti-partition. Bennett won 659 votes (5.4 per cent) to Porter's 2,513.[23]

The NSFU's Belfast branch suffered two demoralising developments in 1921. Henry Adair, for nine years an impeccable branch secretary, was convicted of embezzling £150 from union funds. Though the NSFU did not seek retribution, Adair was given four months imprisonment in July 1921.[24] Further embarrassment arose from the NSFU's acceptance of pay cuts imposed by the National Maritime Board. Criticism escalated from its own rank and file, the rival British Seafarers' Union and the National Union of Ship's Stewards, Cooks, Bakers, and Butchers, the National Transport Workers' Federation, and the International Transport Workers' Federation, turning the NSFU into a pariah.[25] As the National Transport Workers' Federation prepared to merge both rivals into the Amalgamated Marine Workers' Union as a more viable alternative to the NSFU, officials in the ITGWU called for a similar initiative in Ireland. The ITGWU's Archie Heron actually had a hand in drafting the Federation's manifesto for the Marine Union.[26] In September the ITGWU opened direct contact with the Dublin branch of the NSFU and the British Seafarers' Union agreed that the ITGWU should admit seamen living in Ireland and act as the agent of the Seafarers' Union in all Irish ports. On 28 September, with Baird as their secretary attending the NSFU's annual general meeting in London, the Belfast branch agreed unanimously to join the ITGWU. By October the ITGWU's marine section was reported to have a sizable membership in Belfast.[27] Between 1920 and 1922, the NSFU's membership fell from just under 100,000 to 60,000.[28]

Baird was already forging links with the ITGWU and had been guest of honour at the 1921 May Day concert staged by the ITGWU in Derry. The occasion reflected the growing divide between the union and the amalgamateds. Of the 34 labour bodies asked to contribute, none replied and it seemed as if May Day would go unnoticed until 'the Girls' Section manfully [sic] stepped into the breach'.[29] Since its reappearance in Derry under Peadar O'Donnell, the ITGWU had advertised its republicanism and its socialism, and become an Ishmael for both, denounced in the local press as anti-Catholic for its socialism and anti-Protestant for its republicanism. It was even accused of being anti-Derry on the ground that its local organiser, Charlie Ridgway, was from Belfast and a Protestant to boot. On one occasion, when accused of having been in the Ulster Volunteer Force, Ridgway told Newry dockers and carters that the Ulster Volunteers didn't want him as he was 'a Protestant like Councillor Baird, Hanna, and Greenspon'.[30] It was a telling revelation of the binary mentality in Ulster. Simon Greenspon was, of course, Jewish. In Derry, the amalgamated-dominated trades council decided there was no need for the ITGWU in the city and refused it affiliation. The May Day concert opened with uilleann pipes and 'the International'. Baird was introduced by Ridgway as 'a Protestant Labourite expelled from the shipyard because he refused to abandon his Labour principles and who had done yeoman work in raising funds across the Channel for the victims of the Pogrom'. Baird's speech urged loyalty to the ITGWU in the nearing storm, and conveyed fraternal greetings from 'the small Labour group in Belfast which had still remained true to its ideals'. Proceedings closed with 'the Red Flag'.[31] In June Baird enquired about getting a job with the ITGWU. Midgley had done the same in October 1920 only to yield to pressure to stick with the Linenlappers. Nothing was available for Baird immediately, but he was invited to Dublin for an interview, expenses paid.[32]

In September Baird joined Nationalist and Sinn Féin councillors in a deputation to Éamon de Valera and members of the Dáil cabinet in Dublin's Mansion House. The lobby appealed to de Valera to prevent partition and pledged their refusal to co-operate with any partitionist regime. Baird said he was against partition as it would divide workers and hand power to those who had driven men from the shipyards. His ideal, he said, was 'one big union for a united Ireland', adding that any weakening on partition would be disastrous as a Labour government was likely in England before long.[33]

The annual conferences of the TUCs in 1921 merely confirmed the hopelessness of the situation. The ITUC opened in Dublin on 1 August. The executive's report applauded the Woodworkers and argued that things would be very different had other unions taken the same action. It was easy for Irish unions to criticise the amalgamateds as they had nothing to lose in Belfast. They were equally remiss where they might have acted. Tom Johnson, secretary of the ITUC, conceded that he had put no pressure on the BTUC. Never one for confrontation, he pleaded feebly, 'Of course we have no right to ask [the BTUC] for any information'. William McMullen, ITGWU Belfast, delivered a message that was blunt and accurate: 'Some people seem to think that there might be a possibility of some of 'the expellees' being allowed to earn a livelihood again in Belfast. There is not the slightest possibility of that....'[34]

In September Baird and Hanna led a 'delegation' to the BTUC in Cardiff. The delegation was effectively the executive of what was now constituted as the Belfast Expelled Workers (BEW). Representing 'the Labour Party and Trades Council', it comprised Baird, Hanna, Greenspon, and Haslett as secretary.[35] A manifesto was distributed to the BTUC delegates, and Baird and Hanna were given 30 minutes to address the Congress. Their reception ensured that the discussion on Belfast would be the most memorable item on the agenda. Baird represented the expulsions as the product of divide and conquer tactics, used by employers to keep wages low and by Unionist politicians to depict the Irish as unfit for self-rule.

> Last July after very careful preparation and skilful organisation every worker in the shipyards and in other works who had the audacity to oppose the 'ascendancy party' led by Edward Carson was expelled from his work... Every man who was prominently known in the Labour movement, who was known as an I.L.P.'eer [sic] was expelled from his work just the same as the rebel Sinn Féiners...
>
> After that outbreak we thought that the great English Trade Unions would come to our assistance. We looked with confidence to the action we hoped they would take, but the Joiners' Union, and the Joiners' Union alone, took strong action...

Baird went on to warn that the expulsions were part of a wider class war.

> For, understand, at the back of this trouble in Belfast you have the intriguing English politicians who wish to use Ireland as a battle-cry in the future as they have used her in the past, and wish to divide you at another election, you, the English electors. They wish to divide you again on the Irish issue, that is the real reason why the trouble has been stirred up in the North of Ireland.

Scorning the 'loyalty' test, to cheers from the hall, Baird said that as a socialist he did not believe in monarchy. He signed off with a statement of the key issue in Belfast and a demand for an embargo.

> I will present my Trade Union card – and I hope it will be a clear card – I will present it at the works gate, and I will present no other credential. Therefore I hope that at the earliest possible moment you will see that your societies are respected in Belfast, that your card is recognised, and that those who refuse to recognise it are dealt with as they should be dealt with. If Belfast intends to form a little back shop in the interests of exploiting employers I trust you will put a barbed-wire fence around it, and refuse to allow them any coal or steel or anything they require; and this will have a far reaching effect. It will go a long way, no doubt, to settle the problem at Belfast, and will be a big influence in settling what you call the Irish question.

Hanna echoed the call:

> We know that for 14 months you have treated the people over the Channel as easily as possible. You do not want to lose your members. But the present situation can only be cured by the solidarity of the workers and if you determine that no more raw material shall go to Belfast you will strike a blow not only for us, not only for the people in the north-east corner of Ireland but possibly when your day of trial and tribulation comes we will be able to help you [in return] for your help for us... You, brethren in the Trade Union movement, are responsible because we are denied the right to work in Belfast.[36]

The BTUC then debated a motion from the secretary of the National Amalgamated Union of Life Assurance Workers, of which Campbell was a member, calling on the parliamentary committee 'to immediately take all steps necessary to safeguard the interests of Trade Unionists denied the right to work in the Belfast area'. It was a perfect smoke screen. Resolute in rhetoric and pious in practice, it allowed the response to be sympathetic and inconsequential. Even so, for Sam Bradley, a NAUL delegate from Belfast, it was too much. The barracking he received suggests there was more support for Baird and Hanna on the floor than on the platform. What Bradley shouted from the gallery amid cries of 'rot' is a matter of dispute. According to the press and the Congress record, he said:

> We have men on the platform this morning who are trying to sow the seeds of disaffection throughout the country. These are not the class of men we want to come in here. I refer to men like Baird, who from the platform has often said 'To hell with English Trade Unionists. We don't want them. We want one big Irish Union'. (Interruption). I want to say in fairness to Hanna that he did not use those words, but Baird has repeatedly used them in Ireland.

Bradley himself was shocked by the press reports, and protested that the words he attributed to Baird were 'To Hell with the English trade unions! What Ireland wants is one big union'. But the distinctions were lost on the journalists, as they would be lost on later historians who confused the syndicalist case against the amalgamateds with anglophobia.[37] The damage was done. Commending John Hill, A. A. Purcell, and Arthur Pugh for their report on the expulsions, Bradley argued that the Amalgamated Society of Woodworkers could end the problem in 24 hours by settling with the dissident joiners. More controversially, he implied the BTUC was pushing Belfast men into 'Ulster' trade unionism: 'The workers in Belfast say "To hell with the English trade unions"', he warned. Several EWRC delegates spoke passionately from the floor of being hounded and badgered in Belfast to subscribe to documents and of a 'wicked, unscrupulous Ulster vendetta' that had transformed the social and industrial life of the city.[38]

There was outrage in Belfast. Having reported the debate on 7 September, the *Belfast Telegraph* re-wrote its account the next day to make its position clearer. It illustrates how Baird and Hanna were being turned into villains back home:

'DRIPPING WITH BLOOD'
HOW BELFAST IS VILIFIED
MORE OF THE CARDIFF SPEECHES

Councillor James Baird and Mr. John A. Hanna had an innings after their own heart at the Trades Congress in Cardiff on Wednesday when vilifying Belfast in their address on behalf of the 'expelled workers. Here are further samples of Councillor Baird's oratory: -

'The real object of the capitalists in the North of Ireland in fostering religious differences is to break trade unionism, and represent Irishmen to the British people as unable to manage their own affairs'.

'There is some sort of pledge of loyalty to the King or Carson which Belfast workers are supposed to sign before they can get employment.'

'As a believer in the Socialist Commonwealth I will never sign any pledge of loyalty to any King or Monarchy as a condition of being graciously permitted to earn my bread'.

Mr. John A. Hanna introduced himself as loyalist to his own class and a rebel to the ruling class. The hands of the Loyalists of Belfast to-day are dripping with the blood of the men of Belfast. He suggested a boycott of Belfast in the matter or raw material to cure the 'evil'. They had been brought into the trade union movement and were now denied the right to work in Belfast, notwithstanding that they went to church once every Sunday, unlike the majority of people in Belfast, who went only once a year.[39]

Determined to turn them into pantomime villains, the *Telegraph* editorialised:

Councillor Baird and John A. Hanna 'took the flure' to metaphorically twirl their shillelaghs and utter whilaloos in the most approved Hibernian fashion. British trade union audiences have become accustomed to these twin entertainers, and permit them to provide a comic turn when things are turning a bit dull. Councillor Baird is obsessed with the belief that all who hold views different to his own are victims of the 'boss class' or 'intriguing English politicians' or the 'ascendancy gang'. These are phrases which, though they have no relation to fact, rumble pleasantly to the long-eared and long-haired brigade amongst whom he is a burning and a shining light... Belfast workers know Councillor Baird by experience...He knows exactly what they think of his ridiculous performance of appearing in the City Hall in dongarees...[40]

The UULA promptly passed a resolution condemning Baird and Hanna for attempting to 'lower the prestige of our city in the eyes of the United Kingdom'. The Belfast committee of the FEST wrote to the Belfast Labour Party demanding a statement of its policy on their members' call for an embargo.[41]

For its part, the BTUC had not changed since 1920. Lowe was more convinced than ever in the analysis he had offered at Portsmouth and urged an embargo, insisting that by stopping raw materials to Belfast 'we will bring to heel the people who attack the genuine workers'. John Beard, president of the Workers' Union, begged Congress to leave Belfast alone, pleading that pressure would 'help on the cry that has been in the forefront of one programme to the effect that Belfast men should be in Belfast Trade Unions'. The 'Carsonian organisations' would then lead to 'the destruction of British trade unions in the North of Ireland'.[42] The Beard/Baird similarity led to some confusion in the press.[43] The formative intervention came from Hill, Purcell, and Pugh. Hill offered a gesture to Baird, who had reprimanded boilermakers objecting to his controversial intervention in the 1907 by-election in Belfast.

The key of the situation is the difference in the method between the Executive of the Woodworkers' Union and the methods of the executives of the other unions concerned in the present dispute. Mr Baird tells you that had the other executives taken the same action as the Joiners' Executive the matter would have been immediately solved. Whether that is correct or not I am not going to argue...

And that was as much as Baird and Hanna were going to get. Baird's prescription was 'no solution now', said Hill. He, Purcell, and Pugh stood by the approach they had taken in 1920, arguing that the Amalgamated Society of Woodworkers had taken precipitate action in expelling members, and that the path to a general settlement lay through resolving the split within the Woodworkers.[44] Another reason for the trio's caution was that the renegade joiners' vigilance committee had taken a case to the High Court, contending that the Woodworkers' executive had acted ultra vires. The dispute dragged on until 18 September 1922 when Hill and the FEST secretary brokered a deal. The renegades agreed that 'recognition of the trade union card be the only credential necessary to obtain and follow employment', but their provisional committee came to control the Woodworkers in Belfast. Very few of the carpenters or other expelled men got their jobs back.[45] At the close of the congress Simon Greenspon took up a collection which realised £16.5s.[46]

Ultimately, as the speeches by Hanna and Beard suggested, the BTUC's reticence was dictated by vested interests. Keeping members was the bottom line. Beard's Workers' Union and the NAUL were quite prepared to confront loyalists when the Ulster Workers' Union tried to poach in the shipyards. Oblivious to its own concessions to loyalists, the NAUL described it as 'only a Trades Union in name...in reality a political Union got up to perpetuate the recent trouble and to prevent men from working unless holding their own political views'.[47]

Baird and Hanna stayed on in Britain to address meetings in England and Wales, and speak in London's Trafalgar Square on Sunday 16 October with the legendary Tom Mann. 'To the Square', urged the *Daily Herald* in an editorial, endorsing the Baird/Hanna view that the expulsions were engineered by big business to divide and conquer in what the *Herald* called 'Hellfast'. 'Copper, silver, and one or two Treasury notes were showered on the plinth of the Nelson column', noted the *Northern Whig* with disgust. Baird was still campaigning in London to the end of the year and again spoke in Trafalgar Square on 11 December with Hanna and T. A. Jackson, the Communist Party of Great Britain's Irish expert. Just back from Ireland, Jackson made 'a rousing speech' in favour of a workers' republic. Over 1,000 Londoners attended. Before Christmas Baird spoke 'with several Labour MPs' under the auspices of Deptford trades council.[48] Unionists were motoring on with more of the same. In November 1921 elements in the UULA helped to cement the new realities by organising another loyalist force, the Ulster Imperial Guards.[49]

LIAISING WITH REPUBLICANS

The impact of Baird and Hanna led to renewed interest among republicans in the labour question, and attracted the attention of Peter Keating. Born in Athenry, the sixty-year-old Keating was now a director of J. W. Hey, a paper and box import-export agency in Holborn, friendly with the Communist MP Shapurji Saklatvala, and keen to link the Irish cause with the British left and anti-imperialism.[50] He was also watched by Scotland

Yard for suspected financing of arms for the Riffs in Spanish Morocco. On 31 October Keating told Art O'Brien, founder of the Irish Self Determination League and Dáil Éireann's representative in London, that he had met Baird and Hanna, found them honest, informed, and well-able for heckling, and that use might be made of them to explain that what was happening in Ulster was not inter-communal sectarianism but a pogrom. They had the added advantage, Keating said, of being Protestants. Keating suggested meetings be held in 18 London boroughs with strong Labour Parties, and was confident that Ulster would draw 'large and middle-class crowds'. With 27 branches in London, the League would have been an asset and of financial value, but O'Brien was not keen on association with Labour or leftists and was pre-occupied with the negotiations for the Anglo-Irish treaty.[51] Nonetheless, Baird went ahead with talks to Labour Party meetings in Fulham, Deptford, Plumstead, and Saint Pancras. New possibilities opened when O'Brien was replaced as Dáil representative for his opposition to the Anglo-Irish treaty. By now back in Belfast and bed-ridden with illness, Baird wrote to O'Brien's successor, C. B. Dutton, on 9 January 1922 and received a prompt and positive reply. He immediately left for London and asked Dutton to subvent further meetings and printed propaganda. He also urged that Irishmen press their union branches to commit financially to the cause, noting astutely, 'when you induce men to put cash into anything, you have them...'. Dutton responded positively.[52]

The Craig-Collins pact on 21 January 1922, when Michael Collins promised to suspend the Belfast Boycott in return for Craig's commitment to endeavour to get the expelled workers re-instated, put an end to the campaign in England. Baird wrote to Keating on 27 January saying it was pointless to continue and declining further funding, but hoping the Self-Determination League would persist as 'we want the English public opinion so educated that when Ireland once again proclaims a republic, England will recognise it, not crush it in blood'.[53] Clearly, he did not see the Anglo-Irish treaty as a final settlement, and regretted the termination of the BEW in Britain:

> We were here on a charitable mission representing Trade Unionism and Labour, every Branch of every trade union, also every Labour Party and Trades Council open to us, had a unique opportunity to put Ireland's case for independence before the people we must win over before an Irish republic can function in peace.
>
> Had we received the assistance of the I.S.D.L. we could have done ten times the work and now...the opportunity is lost forever.[54]

Keating thought highly of Baird's ability but was more sceptical about his motives. He advised Dutton that 'these Ulster propagandists' be utilised as 'we cannot leave Ulster as she is', they would do good work 'smashing the workers and the non-conformies faith in Ulster'. Baird continued to speak occasionally in London, and Keating asked if he wished to join a team of six speakers for a propaganda blitz in England, with the six speaking at six different venues each night. Hanna and veteran socialist republican Danny McDevitt were also to be involved. Baird demurred, saying he was reluctant to take a leading role as some suspected him of hustling for a job from Keating, while others had warned him he was putting himself at risk by staying in Belfast. Keating reckoned this was just a bargaining ploy and believed him to be 'a bit of a jealous chap' and anxious to be 'the star'. He also surmised that Baird was angling for higher fees than the other speakers and offered him the possibility of additional earnings from expenses, though Baird said he would speak without any guarantees about money. With no enthusiasm for an initiative that might not chime with the Provisional Government's Northern policy, Dutton temporised.[55]

Whatever the truth of Keating's suspicions, Baird was genuinely worried about the worsening situation in Belfast. The Craig-Collins pact was not delivering. Asked to lobby the Provisional Government, Johnson assured the BEW that Collins would involve them in any discussions on the expellees.[56] On 2 February Baird and Haslett arrived at Dublin City Hall shortly after Craig in the hope of an audience with himself and Collins, and waited in vain. They were seen instead by Joseph McGrath, Minister for Labour in the Provisional Government. Baird complained that while the boycott had been lifted, shipyardmen had recently assaulted a group of electricians who attempted to go back to work. Disappointed, he and Haslett returned home.[57] A crisis loomed with the possible termination of White Cross money. On its formation, the White Cross had found that some 30,000 people in Belfast were on the verge of starvation and the Belfast Expelled Workers' Fund had virtually exhausted its sources. It took up the slack, paying the fund £5,000 per week until November 1921, when the grant was increased in response to further demands.[58] The BEW was now dependent totally on the White Cross and both operated out of McDevitt's address at 5 Rosemary St after the military commandeered Saint Mary's Hall and confiscated White Cross papers. It was an uncomfortable position for Baird as elements on the almost entirely Catholic White Cross committee opposed any recognition of the Northern regime, whereas he wished to pursue a more pragmatic line through the Belfast Labour Party.[59]

The strain began to tell. Hastening to Dublin for another meeting with McGrath on 24 February 1922, Baird vented his frustration to 'comrade' Keating:

few people in the south seem to understand <u>how</u> to deal with 'Ulster'. At least half the Catholic people of Belfast <u>must</u> be provided for, for some time (possibly a long time to come) and the White Cross ceases to function in about eight weeks. £100,000 will be earmarked for Belfast. I am convinced that if done in a business like way cash to <u>build</u> up industries could be raised in the States bonds could be sold on lines similar to those adopted by De Valera…our people are getting despondent and just a little demoralized few Irish politicians realize that the 'Papes' in Belfast have always had to bear punishment for the shooting of landlords the talk of Home Rule 'Sinn Féin' <u>murders</u> etc etc vengeance was taken against <u>them</u> no matter what happened elsewhere they have a right to the protection of the new government and of every man in the Free State. I have been 'on the mat' a sort of Irish mendicant for a year and eight months I am getting tired I feel I have accomplished so little. [as in the original].[60]

McGrath was non-committal, but the BEW was revamped in early March. Baird presided over a 'very large' meeting of expelled women workers in the Foresters' Hall in Belfast's Divis Street, where Greenspon delivered a report, and over another 'thronged' meeting of expelled men that demanded the implementation of the Craig-Collins pact.[61] Though timorous and living in a state of terror, not knowing what might happen next, the Belfast Labour Party remained Baird's organisation of choice, and he led a delegation from the party, comprising himself, Haslett, and Greenspon, to meet Craig, Sir Richard Dawson Bates, Minister of Home Affairs, and J. M. Andrews, Minister of Labour and president of the UULA, on 21 March. The White Cross was not informed, and Baird worried about the financial consequences. The Prime Minister, the most moderate of the three, offered little comfort, reiterating his backing for the 'pogrom'. He had consulted with the men behind the expulsions and said they agreed to take the expellees back as vacancies arose, provided ex-servicemen were given preference and three loyalists were hired for every one expelled man. Craig denied his government had any intention of making special provision for expellees, but was prepared to approach the British treasury to get grants for relief.

The Craig-Collins pact went unfulfilled – Collins repudiated but could not unmake the boycott entirely and destruction of Belfast goods persisted in the 26 counties, Craig cited the Boundary Commission as the latest source of loyalist insecurity, and both realised they had profoundly different expectations of a border revision. Craig was startled when Collins showed him a map indicating the transfer of Fermanagh, Tyrone, Derry City, and chunks of Armagh and Down to the Free State. Concluding, Craig told the Labour delegates that 'there was no hope of carrying out any of the assurances he had given to Mr Collins so long as non-recognition was the policy of the minority'.[62] Writing to Keating, Baird summed up the dilemma of his people: 'in a word we are hostages of war placed in enemy country, without rights, and our friends in Southern Ireland are so busy playing the political game they have no time to consider our case'. He signed off 'Yours in a gloomy mood'. Like many Northerners, the only leader in whom he had any faith was Collins, and he asked that his report on the interview with Craig be forwarded to him.[63] His confidence may have been misplaced. Collins repeatedly put off meeting him. Assessing the wider picture, Baird anticipated the defeat of the Unionists in the next Westminster election, and said he was willing to continue working with the Dublin and Belfast governments, but believed the expelled workers would get justice only in an Irish republic.[64]

The last hope for the expelled workers arose from the grisly 'McMahon massacre', the killing of six members of the family of businessman Owen McMahon on 24 March. The Labour Party and Trade Union Congress executive resolved to interview the Dáil cabinet to seek the reinstatement of the boycott in view of the failure to get expelled men back to work and intensified attacks on Catholics. Alarmed at rumours of police involvement in the McMahon murders, and their potential for destabilising the Anglo-Irish Treaty, Colonial Secretary Winston Churchill agreed to demands from Collins that another meeting be arranged with Craig. A second Craig-Collins pact was signed in London on 30 March. Thanks to Joe Devlin, MP, and wealthy Catholics who favoured a compromise with the Northern state, it was more specific on expelled workers. The Northern signatories to the pact promised 'every effort to secure the restoration of the expelled workers'. Where that proved 'impracticable at the moment, owing to trade depression', they were to be afforded preference in employment on public works. A British grant of £500,000 was to be given to the Northern Ministry of Labour for relief works in the Belfast area, one third of which was to be earmarked for Catholics. Again there was disappointment. Anti-Catholic and IRA violence continued, and by mid-April the pact was dead. In the heel of the hunt, only a few dozen expellees were reinstated.[65] For the BEW activists, the prospects were bleak. Dutton remained impervious to Keating's appeals for a propaganda campaign in England. Greenspon thought of going into business. Baird suggested he try London. Baird himself felt stranded and was conscious of the strain on his family. He wrote on 4 April:

> There is no hope for the minority in Belfast unless a strong stable government is set up in southern Ireland, the old gang here are doing all the[y] can to stir up a <u>religious</u> war so that the reentry of England may be justified. You could not imagine how insolent and arrogant they are at present.
> Even people regarded as peaceable have no word of condemnation for what is being done.

> Mrs Baird is almost a nervous wreck. Nora my eldest girl is almost as bad and since the McMahon murders I am a bit shaken myself. My second girl [Geneve] sails very soon for Canada, I fully realize we cannot live here even [if] we had a settlement. How to get out or where to go is the problem.[66]

Circumstances must have been particularly embarrassing for Nora who was giving piano lessons in Belfast from June 1921 at latest.[67] She was fortunate that the Belfast music world was pointedly a-political. Noting her regular achievements as a tutor, the press never made the connection with her father.

James had become more active on Belfast Corporation in early 1922 and continued to discharge his duties as a city councillor up to 11 May when he added his name to a letter protesting against wage cuts for municipal employees. On 9 May he attended his last committee meeting in the City Hall.[68] On 22 May, Organiser Baird and 110 roadmen stormed the boardroom of Thomastown Rural District Council to demand that all roads in the area be maintained by direct labour. A very different chapter of his life had begun, with a promising start too. The occupation tactic worked.[69]

CHAPTER 6

Organiser

an agitator of the most extreme type.

Kevin O'Higgins on Baird.[1]

James Baird had met William O'Brien, acting general secretary of the ITGWU, and his executive committee in Dublin on 22 March 1922 only to be informed that the union was cutting back on expenditure.[2] But by May he was a union organiser. He must have been regarded as an exceptional asset to have been taken on. He had of course an impressive curriculum vitae as a branch secretary, local councillor, and public speaker. There was political sympathy for Northern victims, and he had brought the ITGWU a dowry in the form of the Belfast branch of the NSFU. Nonetheless, not everyone was welcome at any price. Peadar O'Donnell reckoned that Derry dockers might have been poached at this time had Liberty Hall been willing to employ their branch secretary, one Bill McNulty.[3] It was not a good time to be working for the One Big Union (OBU), as the ITGWU liked to be known. Fuelled by manpower shortages, the war economy, and a post-war boom generated by the release of pent-up demand, wage rates had improved for most workers from 1917 and the union had mushroomed from 5,000 to 120,000 members.[4] In August 1920 the boom ended. Agricultural prices fell and by 1921 industry was moving rapidly into a slump. By December, almost 26 per cent of insured workers were unemployed.[5] The insurance acts excluded about 330,000 farm labourers and domestic servants who were experiencing even higher unemployment. Employers demanded that wages return to 1914 levels. Britain's 'Black Friday', 15 April 1921, when the 'triple alliance' of the Miners' Federation, the National Union of Railwaymen, and the National Transport Workers' Federation, collapsed and left the miners to face wage cuts on their own, was the signal for a general assault on wages in the UK. Six million British workers saw their weekly pay packets reduced by 8s. by the end of the year.[6] Irish Labour was rattled. Thomas Foran, president of the ITGWU and of the ITUC in 1920–1, savagely denounced J. H. Thomas, general secretary of the Railwaymen, and promised 'no Black Fridays in Ireland'. He even suggested it might be worth gambling all on a general strike, telling the 1921 Congress: 'We may as well all go down together now as drag the thing on'.[7] Baird would later throw these words back at him.

For the moment, unsettled conditions and the lack of policing discouraged a similar 'big push' in Ireland. It was obvious from 1919 that employers could not rid industrial relations of syndicalist style direct action without the aid of strong government, and the anarchy, as they saw it, dragged on. The Anglo-Irish truce on 11 July was followed by months of uncertainty and the formation of a weak Provisional Government in January 1922. About three quarters of the IRA took the anti-Treaty side and occupied most of the barracks evacuated by the departing British forces. Civil war broke out on 28 June, and it was September before the Provisional Government began to establish law and order in the provinces. The Irish employers' offensive began in August 1921, and then stuttered along in fits and starts. The ITGWU was proud of its refusal to follow the amalgamateds and accept wage cuts in line with the process of rapid 'readjustment' in Britain. Driven by the enormous rank and file confidence that had accumulated with the relentless advance of Labour since 1917, and by the leadership's ambition to discredit and dislodge the amalgamateds, over half its members still held peak rates in 1923. But for how long could economic reality be postponed?

While the rank and file were demanding more militancy, Liberty Hall was attempting to deal with the looming crisis by consolidating central control over a union that had grown rapidly and spontaneously, with hundreds of branches, often based on parishes. It reduced its organising staff from 21 to 17 in May 1920. The number had fallen to 11 by May 1921, nine by July 1922, and eight by April 1923 when Baird was designated organiser for 'Waterford, Part-Kilkenny', an area with 24 branches and 3,700 members. People like Baird were on the way out. Séamus Hughes, a former acting general secretary, ousted by O'Brien, claimed that by 1922, because of the difficulty of organising rural workers, Foran was willing to settle for an essentially Dublin union, with a scattering of branches in a few of the larger provincial centres. O'Brien, he conceded, still wanted a nation-wide organisation.[8] In practice, Liberty Hall meant Foran and O'Brien, though both had their desks in the union's 'executive offices' at 35 Parnell Square.[9] Foran had been a docker before becoming the ITGWU's first general president. Gregarious and easy-going, he was happy to follow O'Brien's policies on wage movements and organisation. O'Brien had worked as a tailor but been involved with the ITGWU from its foundation by Jim Larkin in 1909. In October 1914 Larkin went to America, leaving James Connolly as de facto general secretary. After Connolly's death,

O'Brien joined the ITGWU, and was instrumental in re-building it after the disruption of Easter Week. Formally the general treasurer, he would come to rule the organisation with an iron fist. Keen to create efficient and hierarchical management structures, he introduced measures to augment officialdom at local level. Under the guise of implementing the OBU's industrial unionist blueprint *The Lines of Progress*, written by Foran, a 'big branch' scheme was promoted in 1921 with the aim of establishing branches of sufficient size to sustain full-time paid secretaries who would owe their jobs to head office instead of part-timers elected annually. Baird drew praise in the *Voice of Labour* for his persistence in turning County Waterford's 22 branches into three 'big branches', covering the east, mid, and west of the county. There were also full-time secretaries in Waterford city and Dungarvan. Other counties were not so compliant. By May 1923 just 50 of the union's 324 branches had full-time officials.[10]

The increasingly authoritarian atmosphere generated by O'Brien led to resentment. A conference of organisers and Head Office staff in 1922 demanded improvements in salaries and allowances, and bi-annual conferences with the executive committee. The average cost of an organiser was £8.6s.7d per week, comprising about £5 in wages plus expenses.[11] Coevally, the union suffered the embarrassment of a strike by its clerical staff, provoked by tactless favouritism on the part of the executive. The Communist Party's *Workers' Republic* thundered against the 'bureaucrats' and demanded they be 'cleared out'.[12] If the party was of little electoral significance, several ITGWU branches expressed their bewilderment and unease over the strike and urged the executive to settle it at once as it was having a demoralising effect on members.[13]

ORGANISING THE UNION

Operating from Bagenalstown, County Carlow, Baird's union work was mainly in the south-east, but occasionally took him as far afield as Cork and Kerry. It is likely that Frances and the children remained in Belfast. As late as August 1922 C. B. Dutton and Peter Keating were still writing to him at 5 Rosemary Street, Belfast.[14] The south-east was not unknown to James. In 1918 Nora had been affected by the Spanish Flu and sent to recuperate with an aunt in the smogless air of Kilkenny.[15] However, in contrast to the great aggregations of trades in Harland and Wolff, James was now managing the scattered variety of employments that made up the Irish provincial working class: farm labourers, roadmen, dockers, flour millers, builders' labourers, and operatives in bakeries, creameries, gas works, tanneries, and saw-mills among other places. Unlike the Ballymacarrett Boilermakers or the Belfast NSFU, a branch of the OBU in the provinces might contain

men and women in a dozen or more occupations. He was also dealing
with different mentalities. A boilermaker was in a lifelong profession and
knew his life was shaped by the rules of industrial relations and the trade
cycle. A slump would eventually yield to a boom. Whatever happened,
his best option was to stick to his craft and his union. Most of Organiser
Baird's members had never been unionised before 1917 and reckoned a
lost strike could mean a permanent return to the grinding poverty of pre-
war years. Without land, property, or social status, an agricultural labourer
who supplemented his income with odd jobs, occasional roadwork, or
some inland fishing might be more class conscious than a shipyardman,
but he was less likely to feel bound by the strategic interests of the Labour
movement. Yet his expectations were higher and, like all union employees,
Baird was caught between the perceived self-interests of the membership
and the organisation. Coincidentally, the only other ITGWU organiser
in the south-east was his former colleague on Belfast Corporation, Denis
Houston, who supervised Wexford, Carlow, and 'part-Kilkenny'.[16] The
work also led to Baird speaking for the Labour Party in its first, and the
Free State's first, general election.[17]

On top of everything else, there was the Civil War. After the Battle of
Dublin, Munster became the crucible of the conflict and saw intermittent
guerrilla action until the IRA ceasefire on 30 April 1923, when the IRA
announced a suspension of offensive operations and authorised Éamon de
Valera to enter peace negotiations with the government, a gesture derided
by President W. T. Cosgrave. Baird was twice arrested and released that
month.[18] O'Brien was amused:

> He was a very talkative fellow and all that, but the anti-Treaty and the Free
> State troops were active down there and you could not move without a
> permit. He thought he was very cute in procuring a permit from each side.
> On one occasion he produced the wrong one and was promptly arrested.[19]

Occasional sniping and arrests continued. The last fatality of the Civil
War in Waterford was shot by a Free State army patrol on 24 May, the
day the war ended formally. The mentalities created by years of warfare
and lawlessness were not so easily terminated. The internment of some
12,000 republicans gave the Civil War a continuing immediate relevance
and the location of four army battalions at Youghal, Fermoy, Clonmel,
and Waterford meant that there were plenty of troops available – 2,300 in
January 1923 – for deployment in industrial disputes.[20]

Much of Baird's time in the autumn of 1922 was taken up with Carlow.
On 7 October the *Voice of Labour* reported:

County Carlow is now in a tidier condition, from a union point of view, than it has been for the last couple of years...Organisers [Joe] Metcalfe [Bray] and Baird parcelled out the County between them and have swept away a lot of cobwebs...Kildavin has been shook up by Organiser Baird, and he has been active generally in the southern portion of the County.

Allowing for the propagandist nature of the paper, reports on Baird were positive. In November the *Voice* commended him for 'rapidly succeeding in licking things into shape' in Waterford city, and in December it gave his work in Kilkenny a mention in despatches.[21] In April 1923 he was asked to take charge of an intractable farm strike around Athy, now in its 20th week. There is no evidence that Baird led the strike, but Kevin O'Higgins, Minister for Home Affairs, would later write of 'arson widely resorted to' under Baird's direction in the Kildare dispute.[22]

There are glimpses of the cultural difficulties he encountered. Reports frequently noted his northern roots. Leading a deputation to Thomastown Rural District Council on unemployment, he began to speak of Belfast Corporation's relief works only to be cut short by the chairman and told 'Don't talk too much about Belfast. Things are not so nice up there now.'[23] Advising of a forthcoming visit to Kerry, the *Voice of Labour* commented: 'It'll mean a clash of accents, but Jimmy is accustomed by now to acclimatising himself.'[24] Nothing was said, or written at least, about his religion.

Baird's biggest problem was reconciling rank-and-file militancy with the union's increasingly cautious strategy. The strain was evident at the annual general meeting of the Waterford city branch in the Large Room of the City Hall in January 1923. As the secretary read the annual report, some 20 men entered the room with a red flag to cheers from their fellow members. The red flaggers had recently taken over the city's gasworks, rather than accept wage and staff cuts, and declared their intention to run it under worker management. Up to 100 of these soviets took place between 1917 and 1923. Supportive initially, the ITGWU turned against the soviet tactic when the boom gave way to a slump. Baird opened his speech with an appeal to local dockers, currently in the Amalgamated Transport and General Workers' Union, to re-join the OBU and went on, treading warily between his own instincts and his superiors' misgivings:

We have a section of our members here who have taken a big step forward, perhaps even bigger than they know. They have hoisted the Red Flag, the flag of revolt. There is only one flag of real revolt that I know of in the world and a section of our members hoisted that flag here in this city of Waterford. Of course our members of the Press have not forgotten to advertise it, and we certainly have no objection to that. However, as this particular trouble has not yet been dealt with, I need not refer to it further other than to say that the men in the Gas Works by keeping up their end in this will be a credit to their Union, to the workers of Ireland and also to the workers of the world. I think they will do this and do us an honour. I congratulate them on the step they have already taken (applause).[25]

The gas company was operated successfully under workers' control until the army moved in, ejected the employees, and returned the plant to the proprietors on 10 March. The dispute then continued into the autumn as a strike.[26] It would be just one of numerous conflicts in Waterford alone that affected the ITGWU in its annus horribilis and it was a foretaste of the trouble that awaited Baird.

CHAPTER 7

The Last Battles

He was driven out of Carsonia for daring to champion the
rights of the class to which he belongs. It would now appear that
the advocates of economic freedom for the working class will
receive no more toleration from the powers that be in the 'Free'
State than is afforded them in the reactionary North-East.
Democratic programmes and pious resolutions declaring the
workers' right to ownership of the wealth they produce and
the people's title to ownership of the land...how quickly they
are forgotten when these same revolutionaries are placed in
power through the sacrifice and suffering of the workers.

The *Voice of Labour* on Baird.[1]

James Baird's work in 1923 was dominated by the farm strike in Waterford.
Agricultural workers had begun to join the ITGWU in large numbers
during the later war years. The shortage of manpower, combined with the
growing demand for foodstuffs and compulsory tillage orders, placed the
labourers in a better bargaining position. In 1920 they accounted for half
the union's 120,000 members. The farmers too had organised, in the Irish
Farmers' Union (IFU). With the fall in food prices from August 1920, the
IFU demanded cuts in wages. Waterford was well organised in the sector
and had established elaborate agreements on wages and conditions with
the Waterford Farmers' Association (WFA), the local section of the IFU.
The county saw a major farm strike in 1922, mainly won by the workers,
but defeated by the big landowners in the west of the county. Led by Sir
John Keane, the WFA was resolved to do better in 1923. Baird was central
to the decision to strike and his backing for the labourers would put a severe
strain on his relations with William O'Brien and Tom Foran. In many ways
the dispute was a microcosm of the battle for the new Ireland at the birth
of the state. Baird stood for the syndicalist militancy that had powered
the Labour advance since 1917. Foran and O'Brien were pragmatists for
whom the survival of union organisation was the priority. Keane was one

of a number of ex-Unionists or latter-day Home Rulers seeking to find a role in the Free State through the IFU, and just the kind of Protestant the government wished to cultivate.[2] W. T. Cosgrave had appointed him to Seanad Éireann. Cumann na nGaedheal shared Keane's view of the strike as a pivotal contest and was so determined to crush militancy in rural Ireland that it had created an army unit, the Special Infantry Corps, for deployment against labour 'irregularism'.[3] Keane himself had good reason to long for law and order. After the IRA began its campaign of burning the big houses of pro-Treatyites, his mansion at Cappoquin was the first to be hit, and was torched on 19 February. Six other big houses in Waterford had been razed by the end of the Civil War.[4]

As one civil war ended, another began with the return of Jim Larkin from the United States on 30 April. In June, after weeks of harmony, Larkin denounced O'Brien in a bid to reclaim 'his union', as he regarded the ITGWU. His reckless initiative worsened an already difficult situation for Labour. Baird's response was representative of the union's officials.

THE DECISION TO STRIKE

To the ITGWU's surprise, the WFA offered to conclude another county agreement, though it insisted on reductions. The Association had been rattled by the 1922 strike. Although it had enrolled 289 new members during the year, the number of paid-up members had fallen. Ever conscious of the need for government support, whether for policing a dispute or making public policy on agriculture, Keane knew it made no sense to appear indifferent to the state's stretched security commitment, telling the WFA's annual general meeting February of the need for stability, and the paramount importance of upholding the constitution and building the Farmers' Party.[5] The choice facing the union was to accept reductions in return for a joint agreement with the WFA or risk a strike in the hope of maintaining existing rates in individual settlements. Foran pressed Baird to make concessions, arguing that arising from the 1922 action a variety of rates now obtained, making it easier for men to work surreptitiously below the union minimum. Foran also demanded that any strike be approved by all county members, not just those in dispute.[6] The caution met a sceptical response from Baird. East Waterford, he told Foran, was almost unanimous for a strike. Head Office had advised taking a 3s. per week cut in 1922. It had been wrong then. It would be proved wrong now. Baird admitted that about 25 per cent of members were secretly working for less than union rates, but felt that farmers individually could be made to renew the 1922 agreements. Financial membership had improved of late.[7]

On 14 April, Baird reported, a conference of county branches met in Dungarvan and voted to defend existing rates but seek an agreement with the WFA. It was decided that in the event of a strike, west Waterford members would not be called out unless organisation improved. The conference deplored conditions for women servants and boys but felt that little could be done to improve their lot.[8] On 11 May, Foran wrote to Baird rejecting a request for immediate action should negotiations with the WFA fail to end in a bargain. Keep talking, he wrote, citing four crucial differences with circumstances in 1922: the presence of the army and the Guards, the continuing fall in food prices, the fall of agricultural wages in surrounding areas to at least 5s. below east Waterford rates, and the larger number of nons and members receiving less than the official rates. Baird replied appealing for action by 21 May at the latest.[9]

Negotiations with the WFA opened in the Granville Hotel, Waterford, in the afternoon of Monday 14 May, under the auspices of the Department of Agriculture's conciliator, M. B. McAuliffe. The farmers proposed that the (six day) weekly wage for outdoor workers be cut from 35s. to 25s. and clipped further to 23s. in November. Other rates were to be reduced proportionately. Bonuses would be abolished.[10] The talks led to a better offer: 30s. for outdoor workers in summertime and 28s. per week in wintertime; 19s. for indoor men in summer and 17s. in winter. There was no compromise on the demand for the abolition of bonuses. Keane insisted they were a source of constant friction. It was a sore point with the labourers, who looked forward each year to their £2 harvest bonus. 'We admit that it is not a generous wage', said Keane afterwards, 'but it is as much as the industry can stand'.[11] The offer was at the lower end of the scale. The ITGWU was currently fighting a lengthy dispute around Athy against 25s. per week which it regarded as unacceptable under any circumstances. The top rates were usually in Dublin, where labourers had recently rejected a reduction to 40s. weekly against union advice. Another comparator was rates for council roadmen, which were averaging about 40s. per week.[12]

Now the union had to decide quickly. Wage agreements were due to expire within hours, and with each passing day the seasonal advantage was fading. If negotiations dragged on, the sowing would be over and strike action might have to be postponed until the harvest, when success would depend on one, not two, seasonal penalties. The offer was put to the branches next day and rejected, with the stipulation that a strike should commence immediately if better terms were not to be had. Privately, the union considered accepting 32s. per week, but would make this known only if certain the farmers were prepared to improve on their offer. On Tuesday 15th, Foran gave Baird the go-ahead: 'The Finance Committee at their meeting today have agreed to support the strike in East Waterford on your suggestion, as the amount demanded and the abolition of the Harvest Bonus needs to be protested against'. Baird informed the WFA of the position at a second conference in the Granville the following day. The WFA's secretary, R. A. Kelly, asked for time to consult the IFU. But Baird reckoned he was stalling. He had been assured by McAuliffe that the farmers had said their 'last word'. The strike began on Thursday morning. About 1,500 men in 23 parishes came out, mainly east of a line from Carrick-on-Suir to Stradbally. Apprehensive at the responsibility attributed to him, Baird wrote to Foran on Friday: 'Personally I would have preferred waiting for three months before putting up a fight but it would have been impossible to hold the men back'.[13]

The fight began in textbook fashion. The press reported effective picketing throughout east Waterford, preventing the free movement of goods to towns or creameries. The economic blockade soon extended to stopping all supplies, including food, reaching farmhouses. However, in the crucial business of forcing wage deals, things were not going too well. According to a Liberty Hall memorandum, dated 16 May, Baird expected widespread individual settlements within two weeks. Two weeks was about as long as the strike could run without incurring a financial outlay in excess of the annual remittances from the county. Tommy Ryan, a Waterford-based member of the ITGWU executive, was less sanguine and 'more or less' endorsed Baird. But Baird was wrong, and in June Liberty Hall concluded that the strike could not be won. O'Brien felt the best option was to contain the conflict in the hope that the government could persuade the WFA to negotiate. On 10 June, the strikers voted to accept arbitration. The ballot took place in an atmosphere of 'panic' over events at 'GHQ'.[14]

WITH BIG JIM LARKIN

The 'events' were the Larkin split. Deported from the United States in April 1923, Larkin landed back in Dublin on 30 April, still titular general secretary of the ITGWU. Waterford Workers' Council promptly passed a resolution of welcome, but it was no secret that those who had taken command in his absence were not so enthusiastic.[15] Unsure of how such a volcanic personality could be accommodated in the union's new structures, Foran suggested he go on a two-month tour of the branches to familiarise himself with changed circumstances. On Sunday 20 May, he set off for Wexford. In Waterford on 22 May, Larkin spoke in the City Hall with Jack Butler, TD, Ryan, and Baird. He had nothing concrete to offer. As with most of his speeches at this time, he revealed a preoccupation with explaining his absence during the independence struggle.[16] Only in summary did he make some inaccurate criticism of the farmers, caricaturing them as landlords and saying they had locked out their men, and condemn the Free State army for defending them. Before long, he would pay for his neglect of the provinces. Larkin next spoke in Dungarvan, with Butler, Ryan, and Baird, who was cited in the press as 'Organiser Baird, Belfast'. Led by a piper, the labourers marched four abreast from the Town Hall to the Square. Again, Larkin addressed partition and the Civil War, and pleaded with republicans to give up their arms and join the Labour movement; though he gave a little more attention to the strike and was well received by the sizable crowd.[17] By the end of May, Larkin had had enough of the plámás and decided it was time to take back 'his' union. On 3 June, he denounced O'Brien, and went on to confront the ITGWU executive and attempt to seize the union offices in Parnell Square. The executive suspended him from the union pending legal action. Like the bulk of provincial branches and officials, Waterford regarded Larkin's action as dictatorial and sided with the executive. It feared a split in the union and termination of support for the strike. The following resolution was typical of the provinces: 'That this Committee of the Waterford Branch ITGWU pledges its support to the Executive (that has been elected by the votes of the rank and file of the Union) in any action taken to preserve democratic rule & prevent dictation from any quarter'. Similar sentiments were telegrammed from the county branches and Baird threw in his own, slightly barbed tuppence worth in a report on 22 June: 'I see by the press you are back in Parnell Square. Democratic rule must be maintained *and extended* in the Union. I hope the differences soon settle and that Big Jim settles down to useful work' [emphasis added].[18] Ignoring the barb, Head Office abstracted the quote and copied it to other branches. The Larkin split would rip the union in two in Dublin, but scarcely affect the provinces.

ALMOST A TD

From June onwards, Baird became a figure of controversy. 'The land for the people' had always been a cause dear to his heart, and during the wage conferences under McAuliffe's auspices, he said the farmers had no title to their land other than 'English Acts of parliament'.[19] He reiterated the point in an article in the *Voice of Labour* on 26 May. O'Brien was furious and saw him as gifting a propaganda victory to the farmers and threatening his search for a settlement behind the scenes. The strike was now requiring a major security deployment, and from early June there was government pressure on the farmers to compromise. Baird's remarks were seized on by the WFA to argue that the dispute was really about the land.[20] On 15 June the Minister for Agriculture intervened. Again, the WFA rejected arbitration and agreed to meet the ITGWU only if it repudiated 'the claim of its representatives to the effect that the farmers of Ireland do not own the land they occupy and furthermore that they repudiate publicly, and disclaim responsibility for the outrages committed against members of the Farmers' Union...'.[21] The union was ready to condemn all illegalities; land ownership was more complicated. Almost every major farm strike since 1921 had raised the issue.

The *Voice of Labour* had publicised the agrarian policies of foreign labour congresses, notably those in Italy, advocating that the soviet system be applied to the land, with ranches broken up for distribution to workers' collectives. Public ownership of land was Labour Party policy and would be affirmed again at the Irish Trade Union Congress annual meeting in August.[22] With Foran due to speak in Waterford, O'Brien scripted him a few lines of reassurance for the farmers. Instead, Foran declared in Dungarvan: '[I can] not repudiate the statement taken exception to by the farmers that they do not own their lands. That was one of the doctrines of James Connolly, that the land belonged to the people of Ireland.'[23] Baird made a concession, of sorts. The ITGWU organised a campaign of 20 meetings in which he and others 'urged their followers not to furnish the farmers with any material from which they could make propaganda' and to avoid conflict with the soldiers who were workers like themselves, a coded plea to end the chronic violence against farmers.[24] It cut no ice with the WFA.

To capitalise on the land issue, the WFA circulated a leaflet entitled "Thou shalt not steal': Bolshevist doctrines preached in Waterford', in which Baird featured prominently, along with a lengthy statement from the Catholic Bishop of Ross. Accusing Baird of urging labourers to fight for the land, the leaflet went on: 'The present dispute is not over a question of mere wages, but a struggle against the tyranny of Bolshevism....'[25] The strike had turned into a lockout over trade unionism and politics. The national executive of the IFU 'heartily approve[d] of the gallant stand made by the farmers of East Waterford in their fight against the Bolshevik campaign waged against occupying ownership of land under the guise of a farm wages dispute...We believe that the attempt to establish a Workers' Republic...would be disruptive of the social, moral and economic life of the country.'[26] Farmers refused to distinguish between strike tactics and Labour policy because they wanted to change both. At the foundation of the state, there was an anxiety to set down markers. Labour had done spectacularly well in the 1922 general election and was expected to do better in the next. A Labour government was a possibility. Now farmers had an opportunity to drive the land issue off the political agenda. McAuliffe noted: 'Politically the situation has brought the full body of farmers and their sons as Government supporters, where a great number were formerly either against or neutral'.[27]

Baird realised that the forthcoming elections also presented an opportunity for Labour. The government intended to raise a loan on the London markets and was concerned that trouble on the hustings would affect investor confidence. Concluding that 'an atmosphere of industrial unrest, necessitating, perhaps, the presence of bodies of military to prevent breaches of the peace during the elections should be avoided at all costs.', the cabinet agreed on 1 August to request employers to postpone wage cuts for three months, during which conferences would be convened under government auspices.[28] On 3 August Baird made another appeal to Foran for general action:

> The bosses and the Government will crush us section by section but are not likely to risk battle with all the workers, which would ruin their credit in financial circles. By making a stand you may save the workers not yet attacked. A good settlement for all at present in dispute is just possible. The next best thing is a defeat involving every member, even if that did happen the men would soon put themselves in a position to fight again. 'Black Friday' should be a lesson for you. Jimmy Thomas feared revolution and failed to meet the attack of the bosses, and the English unions have since been powerless.[29]

Though Foran had spoken in similar terms in 1921, he now indignantly rejected the comparison with Thomas and affirmed that the ITGWU 'has always been ready to adopt a bold policy but not a policy which would lead to disaster for our members'.

Whatever about Parnell Square's opinion of Baird, the boilerman was popular with labourers in Waterford, and was selected as a Labour candidate for the general election in 1923 to replace Nicholas Phelan. Phelan, a former ITGWU full-time secretary, had been expelled from the parliamentary Labour Party in March for non-attendance.[30] Like Labour nationally, Phelan and Butler, secretary of the Dungarvan ITGWU, did well in 1922.

7.1 *General election, Waterford-Tipperary East, 16 June 1922*

Candidate	Affiliation	First preferences	%	Seat won
Dr Vincent White, TD	Sinn Féin pro-Treaty	6,778	19.9	1st
John Butler	Labour	6,288	18.5	2nd

Candidate	Affiliation	First preferences	%	Seat won
Cathal Brugha, TD	Sinn Féin anti-Treaty	5,310	15.6	3rd
Nicholas Phelan	Labour	4,370	12.8	5th
Daniel Byrne	Farmers' Party	3,405	10.0	4th
Dan Breen	Sinn Féin panel	3,148	9.2	
Nicholas Fitzgerald	Farmers' Party	2,466	7.2	
Séamus Robinson, TD	Sinn Féin anti-Treaty	1,436	4.2	
John Mandeville	Independent	583	1.7	
Éamonn Dee, TD	Sinn Féin anti-Treaty	293	0.9	
Turnout	62.8%			

(Source: Brian M. Walker (ed), *Parliamentary Election Results in Ireland, 1918-92: Irish Elections to Parliaments and Parliamentary Assemblies at Westminster, Belfast, Dublin, Strasbourg* (Dublin, 1992), p.107)

'It is certain,' predicted the *Voice of Labour* on 25 August 1923, 'that the Labour Party in the new Dáil will be considerably stronger'. Like all the bien pensants, the *Voice* expected republican candidates to be punished for their lack of a social programme and their wanton destructiveness in the Civil War. Having underestimated its political support in 1922, Labour now erred in the other extreme. Whereas in 1922 Labour was the alternative to continued Sinn Féin dictatorship, 1923 was when Ireland became a democracy, the elections for the fourth Dáil being the first to be free of intimidation and give the people the government that most of them wanted. Critically, the continued detention of IRA prisoners kept national feeling on the boil. Republicans regarded Labour as the soft underbelly of the Free State and attacked it venomously. In Waterford, Labour was squeezed too from the other end of the political spectrum by Captain William Redmond, Vice-President of the Legion of Irish Ex-Servicemen and a champion of Waterford's 2,000 British army veterans. The biggest selling local newspaper, the *Munster Express,* gave him generous coverage, while the *Waterford News* championed Mrs Brugha, widow of Cathal Brugha. The smaller circulation *Waterford Star* and *Dungarvan Observer* were pro-Treaty. The *Waterford Standard* spoke for the commercial and ex-Unionist interests. Labour credibility suffered also from Larkin's savage attacks on the party leadership. However, the major issue for workers was the industrial war, now entering its final phase. Since July, a national dock strike had been damaging the export economy. Dublin was hit by strikes of druggist's assistants, canalmen, and chemical workers. On 21 August, the Cork Employers' Federation locked out 6,000 men in building, manufacture, distribution, and transport. About 20,000 workers were affected directly by the autumn crisis.[31] Labour was losing. Trade unions seemed incapable of defending the post war gains. Debates in Dáil Éireann seemed irrelevant, and the disorder endless. In Waterford the port was virtually closed and the city remained without gas. Dungarvan had been paralysed by a general strike for weeks. Arguably the disruption alienated moderates and the lack of militancy disillusioned the stalwarts. The *Irish Times* thought so in assessing Baird's prospects:

> James Baird has made himself conspicuous by the extreme bitterness of his speeches in the past few months. These speeches may get the votes of agricultural workers in East Waterford, but it is doubtful whether they will have a like success among the trade unionists of the city or the West Waterford workers.[32]

The London *Times* man in Waterford also singled out Baird:

> The language of local Labour leaders has been dangerously violent. At a meeting held recently at Tramore one, after reminding his auditors that they had neither clothes, capital, nor comforts, added, drawing a matchbox from his pocket, 'but ye have these' – an incendiary remark with a vengeance. At the abortive conference which preceded the strike Mr J. Baird...declared that no Irish farmer, great or small, had any right or title to the land he held other than Act of the English Parliament – a statement which in land-hungry Ireland could only be construed in one way by landless men.[33]

Farmers reacted with 'White Guardism', as it was described by the *Voice of Labour* and by some farmer vigilantes. Days before polling, the Knockboy parish secretary was assaulted and had his cottage furniture set ablaze.[34] The election heightened tension in the farm strike, and the strike probably contributed to the relatively high turnout, over 70 per cent against the national average of 61 per cent. Long queues formed at the polling stations in Waterford city. Counting began on 28 August in the City Hall, and when the first count was completed just after midnight, it was agreed to continue through the night. The results were announced at 8am on 29 August.[35]

To the pundits' surprise, Sinn Féin did very well and Labour tanked. 'Astonishing republican successes' ran the headline in the *Manchester Evening News*.[36] As a verdict on the conduct of the farm strike the results were bad news for Liberty Hall. The Farmers' Party vote was down slightly on 1922 but their transfers indicated improved solidarity. The Labour vote fell sharply, and Butler's tally slumped but the more militant Baird polled well.

7.2 *General election, Waterford, 27 August 1923*

Candidate	Affiliation	First preferences	%	Seat won
Caitlín Brugha	Republican	8,265	25.4	1st
William Redmond	Independent	6,441	19.8	2nd
Dr Vincent White, TD	Cumann na nGaedheal	4,059	12.5	
James Baird	Labour	3,186	9.8	
Nicholas Wall	Farmers' Party	3,142	9.7	4th
Jack Butler	Labour	2,710	8.3	3rd
Garret Flavin	Farmers' Party	2,280	7.0	
Richard Keane	Independent	1,741	5.4	
Michael Brennock	Cumann na nGaedheal	735	2.3	
Turnout	70.1%			

(Source: Walker, *Parliamentary Election Results in Ireland, 1918-92*, p.115)

Baird lost by a whisker. After picking up 517 of Mrs Brugha's surplus of 1,751 votes, he fared poorly in winning transfers from other candidates, as had been the case in the municipal elections in Belfast. On the sixth count, the distribution of Redmond's surplus, Baird fell 12 votes behind Butler. Those 12 votes denied him a seat in Dáil Éireann. With only Baird, Butler, White, and Wall, left in the race for the final two vacancies, Baird was eliminated and 3,310 of his 3,434 transferable votes went to Butler, who took the third seat.[37]

Chewing over the crushing disappointment nationally, the *Voice* harangued 'the apathetic throng':

> You are destined forever to crawl on your belly –
> Cling close for your life to the slime of the earth.
> The Matador knows that your horns are of jelly,
> And to-morrow he'll stab you for all you are worth![38]

From the outset, both sides believed that security was critical to the outcome of the strike. On 1 June, in fulfilment of an undertaking given to the farmers by Kevin O'Higgins, 250 troops of the Special Infantry Corps arrived in Waterford from the Curragh.[39] By the end of the month, over 600 Special Infantrymen were billeted in a chain of posts throughout Waterford. They guarded property, escorted convoys, protected scabs, and searched for arms and ammunition. The labourers continued with their arson and sabotage. Martial law was declared and a curfew imposed on 1 July.

After the election, there was a resurgence of 'White Guardism' with a campaign of terror against ITGWU parish secretaries. The strike committee asked how vigilantes could travel about in motors during the curfew? The authorities had questioned no one about White Guard atrocities and made just one arrest relating to terrorism.[40] Baird, for it was he, was lifted by the Civic Guard at the ITGWU office at 1 Lady Lane, Waterford on 6 September. The arrest was made under the Public Safety (Emergency Powers) Act. No charge was preferred, but it was widely assumed to be for advocating incendiarism. It was Baird who made the speech at Tramore noted by the London *Times* man. O'Higgins later confirmed, in response to a parliamentary question from Butler, that he had signed his detention order for suspicion of conduct likely to incite arson. After internment in the makeshift prison camp created for the strike in Waterford Court House grounds, Baird was taken to Kilkenny gaol under military custody. Visitors were forbidden to discuss trade union matters with him. White Guardism escalated after the arrest.[41] O'Brien was not sorry to see his troublesome boilermaker out of the way and had him replaced with Denis Houston, a man with a reputation for getting results. Houston tried hard to get the ITGWU off the hook of the land issue, but the WFA kept going back to Baird's alleged statements and refused to negotiate with the ITGWU.[42]

The arrest brought protests from ITGWU branches throughout the country. That in Glin, County Limerick, called for a general strike for the release of 'Organiser Baird and all the other Irish political prisoners'.[43] The Mountmellick branch also linked Baird's plight with republicans and extended sympathy to the Lemass family on the 'foul murder of their patriotic son' Noel.[44] Captain Lemass had abandoned armed struggle before he was abducted by Free State agents in July. Three months later his mutilated body was found in the Dublin mountains. The case illustrated the dark side of state practice and why popular sentiment had swung towards the republicans. 'To arrest the accredited leader of the locked-out farm workers…is tantamount to a declaration of war upon the Labour Movement', ran an editorial in the *Voice*. In Baird's honour the *Workers'*

Republic published the Wobbly song 'Hold the fort', written by Harrison George. Even Larkin's *Irish Worker,* normally vitriolic on ITGWU officials, joined the chorus, eventually.[45] In Waterford, anonymous typewritten notices were received by 'several' farmers:

> Proclamation. Whereas one of our leaders, Organiser James Baird, has been arrested and is being held in military custody without any charge being preferred against him, other than that he urged the workers to defend their rights and refuse to be treated as slaves:
>
> Now we, the army of the Workers' Republic, sealed by the blood of our dead hero, James Connolly, warn the farmers in the strike area that unless our comrade James Baird is released within the next six days we will order the arrest and execution of twelve farmers in the area mentioned. By order O.C. Dated 17th September, 1923.[46]

The notices were passed to the army and military intelligence officers visited the ITGWU office in Lady Lane. Labour was disturbed to find itself being dealt with by the army rather than the Garda, but it says much about the disconnect between the party and industrial conflict that the only protest on Baird raised by Labour TDs in the Oireachtas was two parliamentary questions from Butler.

In Kilkenny, Baird refused to do prison work, such as cooking and cleaning, and was deprived of letters and parcels and held in close confinement for seven days. Although in 'delicate' health, he went on partial hunger strike – taking a little food and some tea – on 5 October. His condition deteriorated rapidly and on 8 October his medical attendant was upgraded from an orderly to a medical officer. After a fast of 13 days, Richard Mulcahy, Minister for Defence and a Waterfordman, ordered his release. By now in a very weak state, Baird was taken immediately to a Kilkenny infirmary, where he stayed for ten days.[47] O'Higgins sent Mulcahy a stiff rebuke, which he circulated to each member of the cabinet:

> It is difficult to understand the release of Baird without any previous consultation.
>
> Baird as you know is an agitator of the most extreme type and in the course of the Waterford strike carried out under his own direction there have been 70 or 80 cases of arson and innumerable cases of sabotage... such a course can result in only encouraging the other hunger strikers and confusing the public mind.[48]

Over 7,000 IRA prisoners, including 350 in Kilkenny, had begun a mass hunger strike for their release on 13 October. Officers of Waterford Workers' Council and various local unions joined republican rallies urging their release.[49] After two deaths and no prospect of concessions, the strike was called off on 23 November. On the previous day, Baird was in Dublin's

Mansion House for a well-attended public meeting of the Ulster Defence Association, a broad alliance of interests campaigning for victims of the Northern violence, who now included refugees and prisoners. Baird spoke along with Captain Jack White, founder of the Citizen Army. In early December, looking hale and hearty, he resumed duties as organiser in Lady Lane.[50]

THAT ENDED THAT

Meanwhile, the strike was costing the union £1,500 per week and the future of agricultural trade unionism generally did not seem promising. In total, the ITGWU paid out over £41,000 in dispute pay in Waterford that year. Nationally too, the picture was bleak and expenditure (£160,427) far exceeded income (£84,122). Moreover, just over 5 per cent of members were in Waterford.[51] On 20 November, ITGWU Head Office circulated an internal memorandum reviewing the situation. Underneath the type a hand wrote 'sanctioned one week'. A conference of Waterford branches met on 29 November.[52] O'Brien recalled:

> It looked as if it was going to wreck the whole union and we had a consultation with the executive about it and they said that it was all over now and we will have to end it. We decided we would stop the strike on a certain date, but we could not give any notice of it because that would give trouble in a variety of ways. Foran and I went down and we saw the representative body and we told them that was the last week they could be paid. You can imagine how they took that. Our boilerman was there and he got up and said that was very harsh. He said his own union – the Boilermakers – had unsuccessful strikes and they went so far as to mortgage their head office premises to pay for their members. I told him that was alright for a Boilermakers' Society, but that only a small number of our members were agricultural workers. We had to take a different view of it. That ended that and we did not try to organise the agricultural labourers afterwards.[53]

The strike ended formally on 15 December.

From the Black Squad to the Black Legend

James Baird remained active in the ITGWU in the first half of 1924. The *Voice of Labour* recorded him attending meetings in Tallow, Goresbridge, Callan, Clonmel, and Dungarvan. On 25 April, as he had done almost two years earlier at the beginning of his career as an organiser, Baird again massed 100 roadmen outside Thomastown Rural District Council to demand the council employ direct labour rather than sub-contracting work to farmers. On this occasion the council agreed to admit Baird alone. He made his case with effect and the council allocated 81 of its roads to maintenance by direct labour and 56 to contractors.[1] At the annual meeting of the Graiguenamanagh branch on 3 May he spoke at length on 'the long cruel struggle which the pioneers of the movement had to go through' and appealed to the young men to carry on the fight. He also dealt scathingly with trade unionists who had 'scabbed at the ballot boxes' in the last general elections and urged the branch to prepare for the forthcoming local elections.[2] Perhaps it was a valediction. The *Voice* of 17 May described him as a 'splendid fighter', well received in Dungarvan, but carried no further reports of him, and he was not listed in a head office circular to organisers on 7 June.[3] For a time he was remembered for his association with the shipyard expulsions, Belfast Corporation, and the Waterford farm strike. In 1924 the *Belfast News-Letter* denounced the Labour candidates for municipal honours as 'an attempt to resuscitate...the element which was represented by ex-Councillor James Baird of Dongaree notoriety'.[4] Though raised by tenant farmers, with a son intent on a life in agriculture, Baird's exotic background in the black squad offered a convenient excuse for the disastrous farm strike. Debating union organisation in the construction of the Shannon Electrification Scheme, Cumann na nGaedheal Senator Patrick Kenny warned Seanad Éireann on the lessons of Waterford:

> One of [the union organisers] was from Belfast, and he did not know, I suppose, a turnip from a mangold. He was a man named Baird, an iron-

worker by trade. Whether it was the lure of his northern accent, or something else—we generally attribute to northerners wisdom that we do not believe southerners possess—the labourers followed him like sheep.

As Labour had been gutted, in spirit as well as in structure by its industrial defeats, it offered feeble resistance to the black legend. 'The man referred to, Baird, is the man who led the strike', said Labour Senator J. T. O'Farrell in response to Kenny. 'Doubtless he was an injudicious gentleman'.[5] William O'Brien echoed Kenny in his memoirs: 'We had an organizer there [in Waterford] who formerly had been a boilermaker in the Belfast shipyards, and one could not expect him to know very much about agricultural procedure'.[6] Like the militancy and radicalism of 1917–23, Baird was consigned to the dustbin of history. Jim Larkin, with his mastery of myth, could turn 1913 into a glorious defeat and a moral victory. His successors were unable to handle the consequences or manage the perceptions of the post-war struggles. Labour preferred to forget.

In Belfast, the Bairds moved from spacious Willowholme Street to a three-bedroom house at Harrystrand, 122 Parkgate Avenue, Strandtown.[7] Nora was doing well in the city with a thriving piano practice, but the rest of the family thought it was time to go. On 10 May 1927, James, Frances, Eileen, Kathleen, George, and Helene boarded the RMS *Largs Bay* at Tilbury in London, bound for Brisbane. James gave his occupation on the passenger list as 'caulker' and in Australia he reverted to his old trade of boilermaking.[8] After some agonising, Nora joined the family from Belfast in November 1927. She and Helene became noted in Queensland as distinguished pianists. Nora was awarded an MBE in 1980 for her services to music in schools and is commemorated in a bursary offered by Griffith University's Queensland Conservatorium. Helene received the Order of Merit of Australia for service to community music in 1996. Peripatetic as ever, the Bairds lived initially in Alfred Street, Graceville, then in Kingsholme Street, New Farm, and later in Grey Street, South Brisbane. James's last address was the more salubrious Coronation Drive, in the suburb of Milton. On Thursday 2 December 1948 he saw the family doctor, E. J. O'Sullivan, for the last time. He died on the following Tuesday, 7 December, survived by Frances and all their children and grandchildren. O'Sullivan diagnosed the causes of death as myocardial degeneration, arteriosclerosis, and chronic bronchitis. James's remains were cremated on Wednesday afternoon after a Presbyterian service at Mount Thompson. The Queensland press marked his passing only in death notices. Belfast and Waterford did not forget, and their newspapers published short obituaries. O'Brien recorded the death in his diary.[9] Frances died in Brisbane in 1955.

There are unfortunate gaps in our knowledge of Baird's biography. Why he became a socialist and a Home Ruler, why he was scarcely active in politics or Belfast trades council before 1918, and whether his political values were influenced by his Presbyterianism or Ulster's all-pervasive sectarianism is unclear. For equally obscure reasons, though he was after all in his late 50s, he appears to have settled into a quiet life as a boilermaker in Brisbane, leaving his stormy past behind him, though Brisbane had a vibrant labour movement. A highlight of the city's calendar since 1861 was the annual May Day parade; that in 1930 featured 40 unions, clashes between communists and police, and was one of the smaller and quieter parades.[10] One of the fruits of Nora's work in schools was the Brisbane Eisteddfod Junior Choir, which always took part in the May Day celebrations, singing its way down Adelaide Street 'with great gusto'. Yet nothing published on Nora or Helene gives any information on their father.

Baird was exceptional in going as far as he did in embracing revolutionary socialism, militant trade unionism, vehement anti-Unionism, and adopting the republican understanding of the Ulster question. But he was typical of contemporary Belfast Labour activists in being a Protestant, in moving to the left after 1917, in being victimised, and in concluding that Labour depended on working class unity, that partition was inimical to unity, and that Unionism was an inherently reactionary force, fomenting sectarianism to smash socialism. Baird's story also reveals that whatever their political views on the Irish question, most trade union leaders, in London and Dublin, put the material interests of their unions first. In Waterford Baird represented the post 1917 aggressive solidarity and its appeal was evident in the vote he received in the general election of 1923. Not for the first time, the forces against him were too strong, and it says much about contemporary values that the de facto leader of one of the biggest strikes in Irish history retreated into obscurity. When Baird went south, the socialist view of the Ulster question and the spirit of syndicalism went with him.

Notes

INTRODUCTION

1. A recent example is Mike Mecham, *William Walker: Social Activist and Belfast Labourist, 1870-1918* (Dublin, 2019), p.194, who also discusses the 'Rotten Prod' concept. Other examples are the excellent contextual monograph Austen Morgan, *Labour and Partition: The Belfast Working Class, 1905-23* (London, 1991), and the influential Henry Patterson, *Class Conflict and Sectarianism: The Protestant Working Class and the Belfast Labour Movement, 1868-1920* (Belfast, 1980). See also Geoffrey Bell, *Hesitant Comrades: The Irish Revolution and the British Labour Movement* (London, 2016), pp.93-4; Alan F. Parkinson, *Belfast's Unholy War: The Troubles of the 1920s* (Dublin, 2004), p.36; Alan F. Parkinson, *A Difficult Birth: The Early Years of Northern Ireland, 1920-25* (Dublin, 2020), p.300, fn.56; Paddy Devlin, *Yes We Have No Bananas: Outdoor Relief in Belfast, 1920-39* (Belfast, 1981), p.47; Arthur Mitchell, *Labour in Irish Politics, 1890-1930: The Irish Labour Movement in an Age of Revolution* (Dublin, 1974); p.125; Marilyn Silverman, *An Irish Working Class: Explorations in Political Economy and Hegemony, 1800-1950* (Toronto, 2001), pp.265-6; John M. Regan, *The Irish Counter-Revolution, 1921-1936: Treatyite Politics and Settlement in Independent Ireland* (Dublin, 1999), p.177; and the insightful thematic review by Christopher J.V. Loughlin, *Labour and the Politics of Disloyalty in Belfast, 1921-39: The Moral Economy of Loyalty* (Cham, Switzerland, 2018), p.48.
2. G.B. Kenna, *Facts and Figures of the Belfast Pogroms, 1920-22* (Dublin, 1922, 2nd ed, 1997).
3. Dan O'Donnell, *Nora Baird, MBE (1900-1991)* (Brisbane, 1992).
4. Wilson John Haire, 'The human history of a shipyard, 1-4', *Irish Political Review*, September-December (2020).
5. Henry Patterson, 'The Belfast shipyard expulsions of 1920', in Emmet O'Connor (ed), *Labour and Northern Ireland: Foundation and Development* (Belfast, 2019), pp.65-83.
6. To distinguish them from trade unionists, supporters of the Act of Union with Britain, whether members of the Unionist Party or not, will be referred to as 'Unionists'.
7. Pat Sweeney, *Liffey Ships and Shipbuilding* (Cork, 2010), pp.40-1. Except when citing the formal title, the modern one-word 'boilermakers' will be used below.
8. BPP, *Royal Commission on Labour, Volume III*, C.6894.X (1893), p.21. The official history is J.E. Mortimer, *History of the Boilermakers' Society* (London, 1973).
9. The official histories are C. Desmond Greaves, *The Irish Transport and General Workers' Union: The Formative Years, 1909-23* (Dublin, 1983); Francis Devine, *Organising History: A Centenary of SIPTU, 1909-2009* (Dublin, 2009).
10. C. Morrissey, '"Rotten Protestants": Protestant home rulers and the Ulster Liberal Association, 1906-1918', *Historical Journal, 61* (3), (2018), pp.743-65.

11. Brian Lacy, *Siege City: The Story of Derry and Londonderry* (Belfast, 1990), pp.199-204.
12. See Connal Parr and Aaron Edwards, 'Breaking from the herd: the "Rotten Prod" tradition in Ulster labour history', *Essays in Honour of Joe Law* (Dublin, 2018); Connal Parr, 'Expelled from yard and tribe: The "Rotten Prods" of 1920 and their political legacies', *Studi Irlandesi: A Journal of Irish Studies*, 11 (2021), pp.299-321.
13. James Greer and Graham Walker, 'Awkward Prods: biographical studies of progressive Protestants and political allegiance in Northern Ireland', *Irish Political Studies*, 33:2 (2018), 167-83.

CHAPTER I – IN THE BLACK SQUAD

1. Seanad Éireann debates, 14 December 1925, vol.6, no.3.
2. General Register Office of Northern Ireland, birth certificate; Griffith's Valuation.
3. *Voice of Labour*, 19 October 1918.
4. Sandy Hanna, 'Yarns from the vineyard', *The Red Hand Magazine* (September 1920), p.29. For the wider literature see L.A. Clarkson, 'Population change and urbanization, 1821-1911', in Liam Kennedy and Philip Ollerenshaw (eds), *An Economic History of Ulster, 1820-1939* (Manchester, 1985), pp.137-54; Michael Farrell, *Northern Ireland: The Orange State*, (London, 1976), p.18; L.M. Cullen, *An Economic History Of Ireland Since 1660* (London, 1987), pp.16-62; W.A. Maguire, *Belfast* (Keele, 1993), p.63; John Lynch, 'The Belfast shipyards and the industrial working class', in Francis Devine, Fintan Lane, and Niamh Puirséil (eds), *Essay in Irish Labour History: A Festschrift for Elizabeth and John W. Boyle* (Dublin, 2008), pp.135-56.
5. BPP, *Royal Commission on Labour, Volume III*, C.6894.X (1893), p.102.
6. BPP, *Royal Commission on Labour, Volume III*, C.6894.X (1893), p.21; Modern Records Centre, University of Warwick (MRC), United Society of Boiler Makers and Iron and Steel Shipbuilders (USBMISS), Registration Book, 1834-1909, Ms 192/BM/2/1/1.
7. John Lynch, 'The Belfast shipyards and the industrial working class', pp.135-56; Sidney Pollard and Paul Robertson, *The British Shipbuilding Industry, 1870-1914* (Cambridge, Ma, 1979), p.154.
8. Lynch, 'The Belfast shipyards and the industrial working class', pp.140-2, 148; Albert G. Hood, 'Shipbuilding for poor men's sons', *Irish Times Weekly*, 29 October 1910.
9. Henry Patterson, *Class Conflict and Sectarianism: The Protestant Working Class and the Belfast Labour Movement, 1868-1920* (Belfast, 1980), p.30.
10. BPP, *Royal Commission on Labour, Volume III*, C.6894.X (1893), p.20.
11. Patterson, *Class Conflict and Sectarianism*, pp.32-3; Austen Morgan, 'Politics, the labour movement and the working class in Belfast, 1905-23' (PhD, Queen's University, Belfast, 1978), pp.54-5.
12. Cited in Lynch, 'The Belfast shipyards and the industrial working class', p.149.
13. BPP, *Royal Commission on Labour, Volume III*, C.6894.X (1893), p.23.
14. Alastair Reid, 'Skilled workers in the shipbuilding industry, 1880-1920: a labour aristocracy?', in Austen Morgan and Bob Purdie (eds), *Ireland: Divided Nation, Divided Class* (London, 1980), p.117.
15. James Connolly, 'Belfast and its problems', in *Collected Works*, vol.1 (Dublin, 1987), pp.233, 235.
16. Working Class Movement Library (WCML), USBMISS, *Monthly Report*, Annual Report for 1920, xxix; TU/BOIL/1/47; BPP, *Report to the Secretary of State*

for the Home Department on Accidents Occurring in Shipbuilding Yards, Cd.7046.LX (1913), p.3; BPP, *Royal Commission on Labour, Volume III,* C.6894.X (1893), p.102.
17. W.E. Coe, *The Engineering Industry of the North of Ireland* (Belfast, 1969), pp.178-82; K.S. Isles and N. Cuthbert, *Economic Survey of Northern Ireland* (Belfast, 1957), p.217.
18. John Lynch, 'Technology, labour, and the growth of Belfast shipbuilding', *Saothar,* 24 (1999), pp.33-43.
19. Connolly, 'Belfast and its problems', p.226.
20. General Register Office of Northern Ireland, marriage certificate; James Baird's death certificate.
21. Census of Ireland, 1901; James Baird's death certificate; Dan O'Donnell, *Nora Baird, MBE (1900-91)* (Brisbane, 1992), pp.1, 37.
22. O'Donnell, *Nora Baird,* p.5.
23. PRONI, Belfast trades council, minutes, 18 November 1905, MIC 193/1; *Irish News,* 20 November 1905.
24. Mecham, *William Walker,* pp. 108, 115; J.W. Boyle, 'The Belfast Protestant Association and the Independent Orange Order, 1901-10', *Irish Historical Studies,* xiii, no.60 (1962).
25. *Belfast News-Letter,* 3 March 1920; 'Rechabitism and women's rights', *Rechabite,* June 1908, pp.112-13; *Belfast Moveable Conference Souvenir Book* (1899); Mike Mecham, 'William Walker: social activist and Belfast labourist', *Saothar,* 43 (2018), p.43. I am obliged to Mike Mecham for these references.
26. *Irish Freedom,* January 1939.
27. BPP, *Royal Commission on Labour, Volume III,* C.6894.X (1893), p.21.
28. BPP, *Royal Commission on Labour, Volume III,* C.6894.X (1893), p.26.
29. ITUC, *Annual Report* (1919), p.161; *Annual Report* (1920), p.157. Congress affiliates often underrepresented their membership to reduce affiliation fees, but the true figure is unlikely to have been much higher.
30. The National Archives, London, Dublin Castle records, CO 904/203/5, File 171, 28 Folios, Simon Greenspon, violent, seditious, inflammatory language. The affiliates are as cited on the FEST's Belfast District Committee's letterhead. The Amalgamated Society of Carpenters and Joiners merged with the Amalgamated Union of Cabinetmakers in 1918 to become the Amalgamated Society of Carpenters, Cabinetmakers and Joiners, but continued to be known as the ASCJ.
31. Peter Gerard Collins, 'Belfast trades council, 1881-1921' (D.Phil, University of Ulster, 1988), pp.66-7.
32. PRONI, Belfast trades council, minutes, 22 September 1888, 12 October 1889, MIC 193/1.
33. Emmet O'Connor, 'William Walker, Irish Labour, and "Chinese slavery" in South Africa, 1904–6', *Irish Historical Studies,* xxxvii, no. 145 (May 2010), pp.48-60.
34. PRONI, Belfast trades council, minutes, 1903-6, MIC 193/1; *Belfast News-Letter,* 2 January 1906; *Belfast Labour Chronicle,* 6 January 1906. The Belfast Socialist Society had been founded as a propaganda agency in October 1905, and claimed 70 members. It would later become the Belfast ILP's Central Branch. *Belfast Labour Chronicle,* 7 October 1905.
35. *Voice of Labour,* 5 April 1919.
36. Little has been written on Wallace though he was regarded as an important pioneer of socialism in Ulster and Britain in the late 19th century. See Patrick Smylie, '"Socialism of the mild type": the political thought and action of Reverend J. Bruce Wallace, and radical politics in Belfast, 1884-91' (MA, Queen's University, Belfast, 2010); and 'A cautionary antecedent: the Belfast career of John Bruce Wallace',

in Seán Byers (ed), *William Walker, 1870-1918: Belfast Labour Unionist Centenary Essays* (Dublin, 2018), pp.15-26.

37. *Northern Whig*, 18 March 1884.

38. *Voice of Labour*, 5 April 1919.

39. PRONI, Belfast trades council, minutes, 3 May 1906, MIC 193/1, reel 4.

40. *Belfast Evening Telegraph*, 2 June 1903.

41. *Belfast Evening Telegraph*, 2 June 1903; *Irish News*, 1 June 1903; *Belfast Labour Chronicle*, November 1904.

42. *Irish News*, 1 June 1903; *Belfast Evening Telegraph*, 2 June 1903.

43. *Belfast Labour Chronicle*, 3 February 1906.

44. *Belfast Evening Telegraph*, 5 January 1906; *Belfast News-Letter*, 8 January 1906.

45. PRONI, Belfast trades council, minutes, 1903-6, MIC 193/1; *Belfast News-letter*, 5 January 1906; Patterson, *Class Conflict and Sectarianism*, p.134. For more on Boyd see Emmet O'Connor and Trevor Parkhill (eds), *Loyalism and Labour: The Autobiography of Robert McElborough, 1884-1952* (Cork, 2002), passim.

46. PRONI, Belfast trades council, minutes, 3 May 1906, MIC 193/1, reel 4.

47. *Belfast Evening Telegraph*, 12 April 1907.

48. *Belfast Evening Telegraph*, 12 April 1907; *Northern Whig*, 13 April 1907; *Irish News*, 16 April 1907.

49. Mecham, *William Walker*, p.163; *Liverpool Echo*, 19, 21 September 1907.

50. WCML, USBMISS, *Monthly Report*, July 1911, p.46.

51. WCML, USBMISS, *Monthly Report*, Annual Report for 1920, p.254, TU/BOIL/1/47.

52. *Belfast Evening Telegraph*, 28 July 1911; *Belfast News-Letter*, 31 January 1920.

53. Austen Morgan, *Labour and Partition: The Belfast Working Class, 1905-23* (London, 1991), p.230; *Voice of Labour*, 21 September 1918; *Workers' Bulletin*, 13 February 1919.

54. MRC, letter from Baird to the USBMISS *Monthly Report*, July 1919, p.29, Ms 192/BM/4/1/46.

55. The official history for this period is J.E. Mortimer, *A History of the Boilermakers' Society: Volume 2, 1906-1939* (London, 1982). It does not mention the events in Belfast in 1919-20.

56. Cited in Padraig Yeates, 'The men 'going into the Convention…did not own their own souls': the Labour movement and the Irish Convention', *Saothar*, 45 (2020), p.27.

57. Catherine Hirst, 'Politics, sectarianism, and the working class in nineteenth century Belfast', in Fintan Lane and Dónal Ó Drisceoil, *Politics and The Irish Working Class, 1830-1945* (London, 2005), pp.62-86; A.C. Hepburn, 'Work, class, and religion in Belfast, 1871-1911', *Irish Economic and Social History*, X (1983), p. 50.

58. Ronnie Munck, 'The formation of the working class in Belfast, 1788-1881, *Saothar*, 11 (1986), p.84. Patterson, *Class Conflict and Sectarianism*, pp. 88-9; Henry Patterson, 'Industrial labour and the labour movement, 1820-1914', in Kennedy and Ollerenshaw, *An Economic History of Ulster*, p.178.

59. Collins, 'Belfast trades council, 1881-1921', pp.272-5. The ITUC became the ITUC and Labour Party in 1914 and the Irish Labour Party and Trade Union Congress in 1918. To minimise the alphabet soup, it will be referred to throughout as the ITUC or Congress.

60. ITUC, *Annual Report* (1919), pp.151ff.

61. Denis P. Barritt and Charles F. Carter, *The Northern Ireland Problem: A Study in Group Relations* (Oxford, 1962), p.141; Terry Cradden, 'Trade unionism, social justice, and religious discrimination in Northern Ireland', *Industrial and Labor Relations Review*, 46: 3 (1993), p.486.

62. Andrew Boyd, *Fermenting Elements: The Labour Colleges in Ireland, 1924-1964* (Belfast, 1999*)*, p.60; letter from Andrew Boyd to the author, 17 June 2009.

63. ITUC, *Annual Report* (1902), pp.24-5; *Annual Report* (1903), p.31; *Annual Report* (1911), p.18: John W. Boyle, *The Irish Labor Movement in the Nineteenth Century* (Washington DC, 1988), pp.312-14.

64. *Belfast News-Letter*, 7 April 1914.

65. John Gray, *City in Revolt: James Larkin and the Belfast Dock Strike of 1907* (Belfast, 1985), p.238.

66. *Daily Herald*, 16 January 1913; Morgan, *Labour and Partition*, pp.127-39 provides the most detailed account of the expulsions.

67. ITUC, *Annual Report* (1913), pp.11, 13.

68. *Irish Independent*, 8 November 1920; *Sligo Champion*, 13 November 1920; Mark Radford, *The Policing of Belfast 1870-1914* (London, 2015), p.151.

69. *Belfast Evening Telegraph*, *Northern Whig*, 31 July 1912.

70. For a biographical note see Bob Purdie, 'Trade and Ulster Unionist: Senator Joseph Cunningham', *Labour History News* 4 (1988), p.6; PRONI, Senator Joseph Cunningham, JP, 'Particulars of my life', D1288/1A.

71. *Northern Whig*, 26 March 1914.

72. PRONI, Carson papers, letter to Carson, 30 June 1919, D1507/A/30/12.

73. PRONI, UULA papers, minute book, 1917-23, D1327/11/4/1; Morgan, *Labour and Partition*, pp.217-8.

74. Emmet O'Connor, 'Persona non grata: Andrew Boyd, 1921-2011', Francis Devine and Kieran Jack McGinley (eds), *Left Lives: Volume 2* (Dublin, 2019), p.99.

75. Donal Nevin, *James Connolly: A Full Life* (Dublin, 2005), p.429.

76. *Irish Citizen*, 27 February, 6 March 1915; *Voice of Labour*, 16 February 1918.

77. Morgan, *Labour and Partition*, pp.252-3; Collins, 'Belfast trades council, 1881-1921', p.288; *Belfast Telegraph*, 7 May 1918; *Northern Whig*, 1 December 1917; *Belfast News-Letter*, 2 October 1918; *Irish News*, 3 December 1918.

78. BPP, *Report of the Proceedings of the Irish Convention*, Cd.9019 (1918), p.46.

79. *Belfast News-Letter*, 11 May 1918.

80. ITUC, *Annual Reports* (1918), p.107.

81. Morgan, *Labour and Partition*, pp.254-7; C. Desmond Greaves, *The Life and Times of James Connolly* (London, 1962), pp.70, 230; *Belfast News-Letter*, 30 November, 11 December 1918; *Irishman*, 31 March 1928.

82. ITUC, *Annual Report* (1919), p.70; *Northern Whig*, 26 April 1919; Boyd Black, 'Reassessing Irish industrial relations and labour history: the north east of Ireland up to 1921', *Historical Studies in Industrial Relations* XIV (autumn, 2002), p.82.

83. *Voice of Labour*, 12 April 1919.

CHAPTER 2 – THE 44

1. David Fitzpatrick, 'Strikes in Ireland, 1914-21', *Saothar*, 6 (1980), pp.29-34; Imperial War Museum, London, Sir John French papers, memorandum from Sir Thomas Stafford and Sir Frank Brooke to the Viceroy's Advisory council, 20 November 1918, 75/46/12.

2. Henry Patterson, *Class Conflict and Sectarianism: The Protestant Working Class and the Belfast Labour Movement, 1868-1920* (Belfast, 1980), p.95.

3. J.E. Mortimer, *A History of the Boilermakers' Society* (London, 1973), pp.102-3; ITUC, *Annual Report* (1919), p.44; *Voice of Labour*, 8 March 1919.

4. Patterson, *Class Conflict and Sectarianism*, p.96.

5. *Belfast News-Letter*, 22 August 1918; *Belfast Weekly Telegraph*, 31 August 1918; *Voice of Labour*, 31 August 1918, 8 March 1919.

6. *Voice of Labour*, 8 March 1919.

7. Emmet O'Connor, *A Labour History of Ireland, 1824-2000* (Dublin, 2011), pp.110, 118; Peter Gerard Collins, 'Belfast trades council, 1881-1921' (D.Phil, University of Ulster, 1988), pp.266, 288.

8. Austen Morgan, *Labour and Partition: The Belfast Working Class, 1905-23* (London, 1991), pp.230-1; *Irish News, Northern Whig, Belfast News-Letter*, 6 December 1918.

9. Mortimer, *History of the Boilermakers' Society*, pp.103, 344.

10. *Evening Telegraph*, 15 January 1919.

11. Ken Coates and Tony Topham, *The History of the Transport and General Workers' Union, Volume 1, The Making of the Transport and General Workers' Union: The Emergence of the Labour Movement, 1870-1922, Part II, 1912-1922: From Federation to Amalgamation* (Oxford, 1991), pp.698-9.

12. Pádraig Yeates, 'The Belfast engineering strike', unpublished paper; *Evening Telegraph*, 15 January 1919; *Belfast News-Letter*, 15 January 1919.

13. *Northern Whig*, 6 February 1919; Patterson, *Class Conflict and Sectarianism*, p.103; Morgan, *Labour and Partition*, p. 233.

14. C.J. Wrigley, *1919: The Critical Year* (Loughborough, 2019), p.9.

15. *Workers' Bulletin*, 3 February 1919.

16. *Northern Whig*, 8 February 1919.

17. *Belfast News-Letter*, 23 January 1920.

18. *Northern Whig*, 11-12 February 1919; *Belfast News-Letter*, 12 February 1919.

19. Morgan, *Labour and Partition*, p.236.

20. *Press Review* (issued by the second section, general staff, GHQAEF), 7 February 1919.

21. *Press Review*, 7 February 1919.

22. ITUC, *Annual Report* (1920), p.103.

23. *Church of Ireland Gazette*, 31 January, 7 February 1920.

24. Census of Ireland, 1911; Yeates, 'The Belfast engineering strike', unpublished paper; Anonymous, *Tales of the RIC* (Edinburgh and London, 1921), pp.253-61.

25. *Belfast News-Letter*, 21 May 1921; I am obliged to Danny Payne, Liverpool, for information on Hedley.

26. *Belfast News-Letter*, 31 January 1919; *Northern Whig*, 28 January-1 February 1919; *Irish Independent*, 1 February 1919.

27. *Belfast News-Letter*, 25 and 31 January 1919.

28. PRONI, Carson Papers, D1507/1/35.

29. *Workers' Bulletin*, 3, 5 February 1919.

30. Collins, 'Belfast trades council, 1881-1921', pp.293-4.

31. ITUC, *Annual Report* (1919), p.181; *Annual Report* (1920), p.157.

32. *Voice of Labour*, 15 February 1919; Terence O'Neill, *The Autobiography of Terence O'Neill* (London, 1972), pp.31-2.

33. *Northern Whig*, 8 February 1919.

34. *Voice of Labour*, 22 March 1919; *Workers' Bulletin*, 3 February 1919.

35. ITUC, *Annual Report* (1919), pp.76-7.

36. Patterson, *Class Conflict and Sectarianism*, pp.92-114; *Voice of Labour*, 22 March 1919.

37. *Derry Journal*, 3 February 1919; *Voice of Labour*, 8 February, 8 March, 5 April, 14 June 1919; Morgan, *Labour and Partition*, pp 243-4; The National Archives, London, RIC Inspector General's monthly confidential reports, 1 January to 30 April 1919, CO 904/108.

38. *Workers' Bulletin*, 10 February 1919.

39. Irish Labour History Society Archive (Dublin), ITUC national executive, minutes, 7 February1919; ITUC, *Annual Report* (1919), pp.44-5, 48, 114, 119; *Irish Independent*, 1 February 1919.

40. Collins, 'Belfast trades council, 1881-1921', pp.274, 293-4.

41. Emmet O'Connor, *Syndicalism in Ireland, 1917-23* (Cork, 1988), pp.173-4; Patterson, *Class Conflict and Sectarianism*, pp.108-10.

42. *Voice of Labour*, 8 March 1919.

43. O'Shannon defended the publication on the ground that it was the first address from a woman candidate to declare for a workers' republic and was a 'historic Bolshevik document'. *Voice of Labour*, 21 December 1918. I am obliged to Helga Woggon for this information.

44. *Voice of Labour*, 19 October 1918; Emmet O'Connor, 'Labour lives; Cathal O'Shannon', *Saothar*, 24 (1999), pp.89-90; ITUC, *Annual Report* (1918), pp.67-8.

45. *Voice of Labour*, 24-31 August, 7-14 September, 16 November 1918.

46. The *Peasant* had incorporated and changed its name to the *Nation* in January 1909, but would be forever associated with what became a notorious example of 'Rome rule'. The *Nation* folded on 24 December 1910.

47. *Voice of Labour*, 21 September, 5-19 October, 2 November 1918.

48. O'Connor, 'Labour lives; Cathal O'Shannon', pp.89-90; *Voice of Labour*, 8 February 1919.

49. *Voice of Labour*, 22 March, 5 April 1919.

50. ITUC, *Annual Report* (1919), pp.44, 74-5.

51. WCML, USBMISS, *Monthly Report*, July 1919, p.29.

CHAPTER 3 – DONGAREE BAIRD

1. NLI, Ó Briain papers, Keating to Dutton, 24 February 1922, Ms 8457/11.

2. Alec Wilson, *PR Urban Elections in Ulster, 1920* (London, 1972), p.11.

3. Emmet O'Connor, *Syndicalism in Ireland, 1917-23* (Cork, 1988), p.23.

4. J. Anthony Gaughan, *Thomas Johnson, 1872-1963* (Dublin, 1980), p.187.

5. ITUC, *Annual Report* (1919), p.162; *Annual Report* (1920), pp.4-9, 157-9; Emmet O'Connor, *Derry Labour in the Age of Agitation, 1889-1923: Volume 2, Larkinism and Syndicalism, 1907-23* (Dublin, 2016), p.39; *Watchword of Labour*, 1 November 1920.

6. Conor McCabe, 'The Irish Labour Party and the 1920 local elections', *Saothar*, 35 (2010), pp.7-20.

7. *Watchword of Labour*, 24 January 1920.

8. Cited in Henry Patterson, *Class Conflict and Sectarianism: The Protestant Working Class and the Belfast Labour Movement, 1868-1920* (Belfast, 1980), p.121.

9. Cited in the *Watchword of Labour*, 24 January 1920; Wilson, *PR Urban Elections in Ulster*, p.47.

10. Headline in the *Watchword of Labour*, 24 January 1920.

11. Wilson, *PR Urban Elections in Ulster*, pp.16, 47.

12. Austen Morgan, *Labour and Partition: The Belfast Working Class, 1905-23* (London, 1991), p.257; Wilson, *PR Urban Elections in Ulster*, pp.32-5; Peter Gerard Collins, 'Belfast trades council, 1881-1921' (D.Phil, University of Ulster, 1988), p.295.

13. Wilson, *PR Urban Elections in Ulster*, pp.24-5, 37.

14. *Belfast News-Letter*, 14 January 1920.

15. *Belfast News-Letter*, 21 May 1918; *Belfast Telegraph*, 18 May 1918; Morgan, *Labour and Partition*, pp.225, 260-3, 288.

16. Emmet O'Connor and Trevor Parkhill (eds), *Loyalism and Labour: The*

Autobiography of Robert McElborough, 1884-1952 (Cork, 2002), fn.39; *Church of Ireland Gazette*, 30 January 1920.

17. Wilson, *PR Urban Elections in Ulster,* pp.16, 28-9; Christopher Norton, 'Worker response to the 1920 shipyard expulsions: solidarity or sectarianism?', *Études Irlandaises,* 21-1 (1996), pp.158-9; *Belfast News-Letter,* 2 August 1920. For glimpses of McElborough's mentality, somewhat confused and embittered but not sectarian, see O'Connor and Parkhill (eds), *Loyalism and Labour,* p.58 and passim. McElborough also notes (pp.30-1), without comment, contemporary efforts to 'replace [Dawson] Gordon with a loyalist'. Though secretary of the Flax Roughers' and Yarn Spinners' Trade Union, Gordon acted as a collecting steward for McElborough's union, the Municipal Employés' Association.

18. Wilson, *PR Urban Elections in Ulster,* pp.56-7; O'Connor, *Derry Labour in the Age of Agitation,* pp.38-39.

19. BTUC, *Annual Report* (1921), p.268.

20. *Evening Telegraph,* 23 January 1920; *Belfast Telegraph,* 31 January 1920; *Belfast News-Letter,* 23 January 1920; *Watchword of Labour,* 31 January 1920.

21. *Belfast News-Letter,* 3 February 1920.

22. *Belfast News-Letter,* 23 January 1920.

23. *Belfast News-Letter,* 23, 31 January 1920; *Watchword of Labour,* 14 February 1920; *Catholic Herald,* 27 December 1919; The National Archives, London, Dublin Castle records, CO 904/203/5, File 171, 28 Folios, Simon Greenspon, violent, seditious, inflammatory language.

24. *Belfast News-Letter,* 31 January 1920; *Watchword of Labour,* 31 January 1920; *Church of Ireland Gazette,* 30 January 1920.

25. *Belfast News-Letter,* 23 January 1920.

26. *Irish Times,* 31 January 1920.

27. *Irish Times,* 3 February 1920; *Belfast News-Letter,* 3 February, 2, 31 March 1920.

28. BTUC, *Annual Report* (1921), p.271.

29. Morgan, *Labour and Partition,* pp.287-8.

30. National Archives, Dublin, Dáil Éireann papers, 'North East Ulster political situation, proposal by Mr Forbes Patterson for a propagandist paper', DE 2/89.

31. *Watchword of Labour,* 28 February 1920; *Derry Journal,* 20 September 1920.

32. E.D. Morel, 'Ireland a nation', *Labour Leader,* May 1917; *Irish Citizen,* May-June 1920; *Belfast News-Letter,* 3 May 1920. Through the Union of Democratic Control Morel continued to lobby prominent figures to speak out on Ireland. Geoffrey Bell, *Hesitant Comrades: The Irish Revolution and the British Labour Movement* (London, 2016), pp.182-3; Mo Moulton, *Ireland and the Irish in Interwar Britain* (Cambridge, 2014), p.79.

33. *Belfast News-Letter,* 3 May 1920.

34. PRONI, Belfast Corporation papers, LA/7/1/CA/2.

35. *Irish Times,* 7 May 1920; *Belfast News-Letter,* 2 June 1920.

CHAPTER 4 – BELFAST CONFETTI

1. Quoted in G.B. Kenna, *Facts and Figures of the Belfast Pogroms, 1920-22* (Dublin, 1922, 2nd ed. 1997), p.21.

2. The most detailed account of the expulsions is Austen Morgan, *Labour and Partition: the Belfast Working Class, 1905-23* (London, 1991), pp.265-84.

3. Alastair Reid, 'Skilled workers in the shipbuilding industry, 1880-1920: a labour aristocracy?', in Austen Morgan and Bob Purdie (eds), *Ireland: Divided Nation, Divided Class* (London, 1980), pp.116-23; Christopher Norton, 'Worker response

to the 1920 shipyard expulsions: solidarity or sectarianism?', *Études Irlandaises*, 21-1 (1996), p.154; Graham Walker, *The Politics of Frustration: Harry Midgley and the Failure of Labour in Northern Ireland* (Manchester, 1985), p.19; Robert Lynch, *The Partition of Ireland, 1918-1925* (Cambridge, 2019), p.93.

4. WCML, USBMISS, *Monthly Report*, July 1920, p.15.

5. Adrian Grant, *Derry: The Irish Revolution, 1912-23* (Dublin, 2018), p.97.

6. *Belfast News-Letter*, 23-24, 27 January 1920.

7. *Belfast News-Letter*, 16 December 1921.

8. Morgan, *Labour and Partition*, pp.270-1, 303-4.

9. Michael C. Rast, '"The mad dance of death": The Ulster Protestant Association in Belfast, 1921-22', https://www.theirishstory.com/2016/02/15/the-mad-dance-of-death-the-ulster-protestant-association-in-belfast-1921-22/#.YR_t7Y5KiUk, accessed 16 August 2021.

10. Morgan, *Labour and Partition*, pp.270-1.

11. *Belfast Telegraph*, 22 July 1920.

12. *Belfast News-Letter*, 23 January 1923.

13. Patterson, *Class Conflict and Sectarianism*, p.140.

14. PRONI, UULA, minute book, 1917-23, 29 July, 7 August 1920, D1327/11/4/1.

15. *Belfast Newsletter*, 13 July 1920.

16. Morgan, *Labour and Partition*, p.269.

17. *Irish Times*, 27 July 1920.

18. Paddy Devlin, *Yes We Have No Bananas: Outdoor Relief in Belfast, 1920-39* (Belfast, 1981), p.47; *Evening Telegraph*, 11 November 1920.

19. Morgan, *Labour and Partition*, pp.271, 288-9; *Church of Ireland Gazette*, 3 September, December 1920.

20. Henry Patterson, 'The shipyard expulsions of 1920', Emmet O'Connor (ed), *Labour and Northern Ireland: Foundation and Development* (Belfast, 2019), p.79.

21. Henry Patterson, *Class Conflict and Sectarianism: The Protestant Working Class and the Belfast Labour Movement, 1868-1920* (Belfast, 1980), pp.115-6. According to a Dáil report, all Catholics were expelled from the shipyards, Henry's, Musgrave's, the Sirocco works, Coombe Barbour, Mackie's, Ewart's, the Linfield Mill, McLaughlin & Ross, Murray's, Barron's, Antrim Clothing, the Franklin Laundry, Cotton's, Gallagher's Tobacco, and Hall & Co. Some Catholics were re-instated in Reynolds's and the Albion Clothing Co. NA, Dáil Éireann papers, 'Belfast atrocities on Catholics, 1920-21', DE 2/353.

22. Keith Harding, 'The Irish issue in the British labour movement, 1900-1922' (PhD, University of Essex, 1983), pp.181-2; Alan F. Parkinson, *Belfast's Unholy War: The Troubles of the 1920s* (Dublin, 2004), p.37

23. *Irish News*, 6 October 1920.

24. *Evening Telegraph*, 26 October 1920; *Report of the American Committee for Relief in Ireland* (New York, 1922), pp.58-9; *Report of the Irish White Cross* (New York, 1922), p.27.

25. NA, Dáil Éireann papers, 'Complete list of private houses evicted, looted and burned out from July 1920 to September 1921', DE 2/353; Kenna, *Facts and Figures*, pp.35, 38; *Church of Ireland Gazette*, 1 October 1920; *Irishman*, 7 April 1928.

26. *Report of the Irish White Cross*, pp.28-9.

27. Arthur Mitchell, *Labour in Irish Politics, 1890-1930: The Irish Labour Movement in an Age of Revolution* (Dublin, 1974), p.130.

28. American Commission on Conditions in Ireland, *Interim Report* (New York, 1921), p.113. The Commission was made up of leading persons from American and Irish-American public life.

29. *Westminster Gazette*, 24 July 1920.

30. Census of Ireland, 1911; *Belfast News-Letter*, 6 January 1920; Alec Wilson, *PR Urban Elections in Ulster 1920* (London, 1972), pp.18-19; BTUC, *Annual Report* (1921), p.270.

31. S. Higenbottam, *Amalgamated Society of Woodworkers: Our Society's History* (Manchester, 1939), p.227; https://www.ictu.ie/blog/2019/11/12/the-belfast-pogrom-extract-from-labourgender-and-c/, accessed 15 September 2020.

32. ITUC, *Annual Report* (1920), pp.104-5; Norton, 'Worker response to the 1920 shipyard expulsions', pp.157-9; Patterson, *Class Conflict and Sectarianism*, p.141.

33. *Railway Review*, 27 August, 10-17 September 1920.

34. Morgan, *Labour and Partition*, p.271.

35. WCML, USBMISS, *Monthly Report*, June-July 1920.

36. WCML, USBMISS, *Monthly Report*, January 1921.

37. ITUC, *Annual Report* (1920), p.102.

38. Kenna, *Facts and Figures*, pp.32-3; *Evening Telegraph*, 17 August 1920.

39. Higenbottam, *Amalgamated Society of Woodworkers*, p.227.

40. Peter Gerard Collins, 'Belfast trades council, 1881-1921' (D.Phil, University of Ulster, 1988), pp.298-301; *Irish Times*, 27 July 1920.

41. Morgan, *Labour and Partition*, p.273; *Belfast News-Letter*, 31 July, 2, 4 August 1920; *Church of Ireland Gazette*, 6 August 1920.

42. *Church of Ireland Gazette*, 6 August 1920; Collins, 'Belfast trades council, 1881-1921', p.300.

43. *Evening Telegraph*, 17 August 1920.

44. Morgan, *Labour and Partition*, p.274.

45. Parkinson, *Belfast's Unholy War*, p.37; Morgan, *Labour and Partition*, pp.274-5.

46. C. Desmond Greaves, *The Irish Transport and General Workers' Union: The Formative Years, 1909-23* (Dublin, 1982), p.283.

47. BTUC *Annual Report*, 1921, p.114.

48. ITUC, *Annual Report* (1920), pp.100-2.

49. ITUC, *Annual Report* (1920), p.106; *Annual Report* (1921), p.3.

50. BTUC *Annual Report* (1920), pp.382-6.

51. BTUC, *Annual Report* (1921), pp.274-5.

52. Kevin Morgan, *Bolshevism, Syndicalism, and the General Strike: The Lost Internationalist World of A.A. Purcell* (London, 2013), pp.46-7, 246. I am obliged to Alan Campbell for information on Pugh.

53. J. Anthony Gaughan, *Tom Johnson* (Dublin, 1980), pp.167, 436-9.

54. Mo Moulton, *Ireland and the Irish in Interwar Britain* (Cambridge, 2014), p.72; British Labour Party, *Report of the Labour Commission to Ireland* (London, 1921), p.64.

55. Modern Records Centre, Coventry, Arthur Henderson, MP, *Nonconformity and Ireland* (London, 1921), 127/NU/S/1/61xiii.

56. Geoffrey Bell, *Hesitant Comrades: The Irish Revolution and the British Labour Movement* (London, 2016), p.87.

57. An ASCJ delegate cited the figures of 2,600 called out and 600 on strike to the BTUC, *Annual Report*, 1921, pp.117; however the *Report* also said that 3,000 had ignored the strike call and the ASCJ's official history put the number called out at 4,500. Higenbottam, *Amalgamated Society of Woodworkers*, p.229.

58. Modern Records Centre, Coventry, Amalgamated Society of Woodworkers, correspondence, 20, 26 October 1920, 78/ASW/3/1/21.

59. Higenbottam, *Amalgamated Society of Woodworkers*, p.229.

60. BTUC, *Annual Report*, 1921, pp.82-3, 109-110, 115-17.

61. BTUC *Annual Report*, 1921, pp.111-5.

62. https://www.oireachtas.ie/en/debates/debate/dail/1920-08-06/, accessed 3 October 2020.

63. D.S. Johnson, 'The Belfast boycott, 1920-22', in J.M. Goldstrom and L.A. Clarkson (eds), *Irish Population, Economy, and Society: Essays in Honour of the Late K.H. Connell* (Oxford, 1981), pp.287-307.

64. NA, Dáil Éireann papers, 'Belfast boycott', DE 2/110.

65. Morgan, *Labour and Partition*, p.272-4; *Birmingham Gazette*, 5 August 1920; *Irish Independent*, 8 November 1920; *Sligo Champion*, 13 November 1920.

66. *Ulster Herald*, 28 August 1920.

67. NLI, Art O'Brien papers, Baird to Dutton, 10 January 1922, Ms 8457/11.

68. *Watchword of Labour*, 14 August 1920; *Northern Whig*, 18 May 1921; Morgan, *Labour and Partition*, p.270.

69. *Church of Ireland Gazette*, 24 September, 1 October, 19 November 1920.

70. *Birmingham Gazette*, 22 September 1920.

71. *Evening Telegraph*, 26 October 1920.

72. *Evening Telegraph*, 26 October 1920.

73. WCML, USBMISS, *Monthly Report*, June 1920.

74. *Irish Independent*, 8 November 1920; *Ulster Herald*, 13 November 1920; *Sligo Champion*, 13 November 1920; on the union see Pádraig Yeates, 'Craft workers during the Irish revolution, 1919-22', *Saothar*, 33 (2008), pp.37-54.

75. *Church of Ireland Gazette*, 1 October 1920.

CHAPTER 5 – HELLFAST

1. *Westminster Gazette*, 4 February, 9, 26 March 1921; *Belfast News-Letter*, 28 March 1921.

2. *Irishman*, 7 April 1928; *Belfast News-Letter*, 31 May 1921.

3. *Belfast News-Letter*, 2 April 1921; *Northern Whig*, 25 January, 2 April 1921; PRONI, Belfast Corporation papers, LA/7/1/CA/2.

4. *Irish News*, 21 May 1921.

5. *Belfast News-Letter*, 14 May 1921; *Irish Citizen*, 8 May 1915; Myrtle Hill, 'Labour lives, no.19: Margaret Taylor McCoubrey (1880-1956)', *Saothar*, 44 (2020), pp.113-16.

6. The one substantial biography of Midgley is Graham Walker, *The Politics of Frustration: Harry Midgley and the Failure of Labour in Northern Ireland* (Manchester, 1985).

7. NLI, Art O'Brien papers, Baird to Dutton, 9 January 1922, Ms 8457/11; *Belfast News-Letter*, 14 May 1921; Austen Morgan, *Labour and Partition: The Belfast Working Class, 1905-23* (London, 1991), pp.260-2; *Northern Whig*, 16 May 1921; *Belfast News-Letter*, 14 May 1921; Emmet O'Connor, *Derry labour in the Age of Agitation, 1889-1923, 1: New Unionism and Old, 1889-1906* (Dublin, 2014), pp.27-8.

8. *Belfast News-Letter*, 14, 19, 21 May 1921; Walker, *The Politics of Frustration*, pp.22, 51, 156.

9. *Irish News*, 16 May 1921; *Northern Whig, Belfast News-Letter*, 16-17, 27 May 1921.

10. *Belfast Telegraph, Northern Whig, Irish News, Daily Herald*, 18 May 1921; Walker, *The Politics of Frustration*, p.107; Peter Gerard Collins, 'Belfast trades council, 1881-1921' (D.Phil, University of Ulster, 1988), p.301.

11. *Northern Whig*, 18 May 1921.

12. *Northern Whig, Belfast News-Letter*, 18 May 1921.

13. *Irish News*, 19 May 1921; *Belfast News-Letter*, 25 May 1921.

14. *Belfast News-Letter*, 20 May 1921.

15. *Church of Ireland Gazette*, 27 May 1921.

16. *Daily Herald*, 21, 26 May 1921.

17. *Belfast News-letter*, 25 May 1921.

18. *Church of Ireland Gazette*, 3 June 1921.

19. *Northern Whig*, 26 May 1921; *Belfast News-Letter*, 16 April, 25, 27 May 1921.

20. *Derry Journal*, 1 June 1921.

21. NLI, Ó Briain papers, Baird to Keating, 21 March 1922, Baird to Ferguson, 4 April 1922, Ms 8457/11.

22. ITUC, *Annual Report and Report of Special Congress* (1918), pp.89-99.

23. *Belfast News-Letter*, 22 November, 6, 9-10, 13 December 1918; *Belfast Telegraph*, 4 December 1918; *Northern Whig*, 5-7, 14 December 1905.

24. *Belfast Telegraph*, 25 May, 23 July 1921; *Belfast News-Letter*, 19 July 1921; *Northern Whig*, 23 July 1921.

25. *Daily Herald*, 6 May, 7 October 1921.

26. *Daily Herald*, 19 July 1921.

27. *Daily Herald*, 17, 29 September 1921; *Communist*, 8 October 1921; Francis Devine, *Organising History: A Centenary of SIPTU, 1909-2009* (Dublin, 2009), p.121; WCML, NSFU, *Annual Report*, 1921.

28. Arthur Marsh and Victoria Ryan, *The Seamen: A History of the National Union of Seamen* (Oxford, 1989), p.306.

29. *Derry Journal*, 18 April 1921.

30. *Derry Journal*, 15 June 1921; *Voice of Labour*, 20 May 1922.

31. Emmet O'Connor, *Derry Labour in the Age of Agitation, 1889-1923, vol. 2: Larkinism and Syndicalism, 1907-23* (2016), p.48; *Derry Journal*, 18 April, 4 May 1921; Anton McCabe, "The stormy petrel of the Transport Workers': Peadar O'Donnell, trade unionist, 1917-1920 in Derry', *Saothar*, 19 (1994), p.47; The National Archives, London, RIC, Crime Special Branch, Reports on the ITGWU, April 1921, CO 904/158/5; Derry City Council Archives, letter from Charles F. Ridgway to Sir Henry Miller, 4 April 1921, letter book no. 50.

32. Devine, *Organising History*, p.109; ITGWU, Annual report for 1921, pp.9-10; minutes of Resident Executive Committee, 17 October 1920, 5 November 1920, 15 June 1921.

33. *Belfast Telegraph, Irish Times*, 29 September 1921.

34. ITUC, *Annual Report* (1921), pp.3-5, 84-5.

35. NLI, Ó Briain papers, Baird to Dutton, 9 January 1922, Ms 8457/11.

36. BTUC, *Annual Report* (1921), pp.268-71; *Derry Journal*, 9 September 1921.

37. See Emmet O'Connor, "'Sentries of British imperialism"? The question of British based unions in Ireland', *Socialist History*, 29 (2006), pp.1-19.

38. *Belfast Telegraph*, 7, 10 September 1921; BTUC, *Annual Report* (1921), pp.276.

39. *Belfast Telegraph*, 8 September 1921.

40. *Belfast Telegraph*, 8 September 1921.

41. *Belfast Telegraph*, 12 September, 24 October 1921.

42. *Belfast Telegraph*, 7 September 1921.

43. *Daily Herald*, 19 October 1921.

44. BTUC, *Annual Report* (1921), pp.273-5.

45. S. Higenbottam, *Amalgamated Society of Woodworkers: Our Society's History* (Manchester, 1939), p.229; Morgan, *Labour and Partition*, p.284.

46. *Daily Herald*, 14-15 September, 30 November 1921.

47. Cited in Norton, 'Worker response to the 1920 shipyard expulsions', p.161.

48. *Northern Whig*, 17 October 1921; *Daily Herald*, 14 October, 12, 22 December 1921.

49. Michael Farrell, 'The establishment of the Ulster Special Constabulary', in

Austen Morgan and Bob Purdie (eds), *Ireland: Divided Nation, Divided Class* (London, 1980), p.128.

50. NLI, Ó Briain papers, Keating to Ó Briain, 3, 9 December 1919, Ms 8460/17; 9 July 1921, 17 July, Ms 8457/11; Census of Great Britain, 1921.

51. The National Archives, London, KV 2/614; NLI, Ó Briain papers, Keating to Ó Briain, 31 October 1921, Ms 8457/11; Mary MacDiarmada, *Art O'Brien and Irish Nationalism in London, 1900-1925* (Dublin, 2020).

52. NLI, Ó Briain papers, Baird to Dutton and replies, 9-19 January 1922, Ms 8457/11.

53. NLI, Ó Briain papers, Baird to Keating, 27 January 1922, Ms 8457/11.

54. NLI, Ó Briain papers, Baird to Keating, 28 January 1922, Ms 8457/11.

55. NLI, Ó Briain papers, Keating to Dutton, 28 January 1922, Southall Labour Party to Bair, 5 February 1922, handbill for Marleybone trades council meeting, 10 February 1922, Baird to Keating, 23 February 1922, Keating to Dutton, 24 February 1922, Keating to Dutton, 17 March 1922, Dutton to Keating, 18 March 1922, Baird to Keating, 21 March 1922, Keating to Dutton, 3 April 1922, Ms 8457/11.

56. *Freeman's Journal*, 3 February 1922; *Evening Echo*, 6 February 1922.

57. *Evening Herald*, 2 February 1922; *Freeman's Journal*, 3 February 1922; *Irish Times*, 3 February 1922; *Cork Examiner*, 3 February 1922; *Irish Independent*, 3 February 1922.

58. By August 1922, the White Cross had distributed almost £750,000 in personal relief grants, half of it going to Belfast. *Report of the Irish White Cross* (New York, 1922), pp.32-5, 76-7, 86.

59. J. Anthony Gaughan (ed), *Memoirs of Senator James G. Douglas (1887-1954): Concerned Citizen* (Dublin, 1998), p.69; NLI, Ó Briain papers, Baird to Keating, 21 March 1922, Ms 8457/11.

60. NLI, Ó Briain papers, Baird to Keating, 23 February 1922, Ms 8457/11.

61. NLI, Ó Briain papers, Baird to Keating, 13 March 1922, Ms 8457/11; *Donegal News*, 11 March 1922.

62. *Derry Journal*, 6 February 1922; *Evening Herald*, 6 April 1922; *Voice of Labour*, 1 April 1922; NLI, Ó Briain papers, Baird to Keating, 27 March 1922, report on the meeting with Craig, Ms 8457/11.

63. NLI, Ó Briain papers, Baird to Keating, 21 March 1922, Ms 8457/11.

64. Morgan, *Labour and Partition*, p.294.

65. Alan F. Parkinson, *Belfast's Unholy War: The Troubles of the 1920s* (Dublin, 2004), pp.234-5; Christopher Norton, 'An earnest endeavour for peace? Unionist opinion and the Craig/Collins peace pact of 30 March 1922', *Etudes irlandaises* (2007), vol. 32, no1, pp. 91-108; Michael Hopkinson, 'The Craig-Collins Pacts of 1922: two attempted reforms of the Northern Ireland government', *Irish Historical Studies* (November, 1990), Vol. 27, no.106, pp.145-58.

66. NLI, Ó Briain papers, Baird to Ferguson, 4 April 1922, Ms 8457/11.

67. *Belfast Telegraph*, 21 June 1921.

68. *Belfast News-Letter*, 4 April, 6, 12 May 1922; PRONI, Belfast Corporation papers, LA/7/1/CA/2.

69. *Freeman's Journal*, 23 May 1922; *Voice of Labour*, 27 May 1922; *Kilkenny People*, 27 May 1922.

CHAPTER 6 – ORGANISER

1. UCDA, FitzGerald Papers, O'Higgins to Mulcahy, 26 October 1923,

P80/729(2-), cited in John Regan, *The Irish Counter-Revolution, 1921-1936: Treatyite Politics and Settlement in Independent Ireland* (Dublin, 1999), p.177.

2. NLI, Ó Briain papers, Baird to Keating, 21 March 1922, Baird to Ferguson, 4 April 1922; Ms 8457/11.

3. Emmet O'Connor, *Derry Labour in the Age of Agitation, 1889-1923: 2: Larkinism and Syndicalism, 1907-23* (Dublin, 2016), p.48.

4. Francis Devine, *Organising History: A Centenary of SIPTU, 1909-2009* (Dublin, 2009), pp.1004-5.

5. James Meenan, *The Irish Economy Since 1922* (Liverpool, 1971), pp.71, 91; J.D. Clarkson, *Labour and Nationalism in Ireland* (New York, 1925), pp.441-2.

6. Allen Hutt, *British Trade Unionism: A Short History* (London, 1975), p.97; Keith Hutchinson, *The Decline and Fall of British Capitalism* (London, 1951), p.214.

7. *Irish Independent*, 4 August 1921; ITUC, *Annual Report* (1921), p.128.

8. Emmet O'Connor, *Syndicalism in Ireland, 1917-1923* (Cork, 1988), pp.142-3; NLI, ITGWU papers, list of salaries, 1920-2, Ms 27041; Organization, 24 April 1923, Ms 27058; SIPTU archives, *Annual Reports*, 1919-24; letter from J.J. [Séamus] Hughes, *Workers' Republic*, 6 May 1922.

9. See D.R. O'Connor Lysaght, 'Labour lives, no.7', *Saothar*, 30 (2005), pp.99-100; Thomas J. Morrissey, *William O'Brien, 1881-1968: Socialist, Republican, Dáil Deputy, Editor, and Trade Union Leader* (Dublin, 2007).

10. *Voice of Labour*, 5, 26 May 1923; Francis Devine, 'The Irish Transport and General Workers' Union in Waterford, 1918-1930', *Decies*, 74 (2018), p.119.

11. NLI, ITGWU papers, Report to Executive Committee on conference of organizers, Ms 27041.

12. C. Desmond Greaves, *The Irish Transport and General Workers' Union: The Formative Years* (Dublin, 1982), pp.313-4; *Workers' Republic*, 22 April 1922.

13. NLI, ITGWU papers, Ms 27041, circular 18 April 1922.

14. NLI, Art O'Brien papers, Ms 8457/11.

15. Dan O'Donnell, *Nora Baird, MBE (1900-91)* (Brisbane, 1992), p.1.

16. *Voice of Labour*, 3 June, 23 September 1922; NLI, ITGWU Ms 27058, Organization, 24 April 1923.

17. *Evening Echo*, 15 June 1922.

18. Emmet O'Connor, *A Labour History of Waterford* (Waterford, 1989), p.182.

19. William O'Brien, *Forth the Banners Go: Reminiscences of William O'Brien as Told to Edward MacLysaght, D.Litt* (Dublin, 1969), p.114.

20. Pat McCarthy, *The Irish Revolution, 1912-23: Waterford* (Dublin, 2015), p.121.

21. *Voice of Labour*, 25 November, 23 December 1922.

22. *Voice of Labour*, 7 April 1923; UCDA, FitzGerald Papers, O'Higgins to Mulcahy, 26 October 1923, P80/729(2-3). I am obliged to Terry Dunne for information on Baird and Athy.

23. *Kilkenny People*, 27 May 1922.

24. *Voice of Labour*, 6 January 1923.

25. *Waterford News*, 2 February 1923.

26. O'Connor, *A Labour History of Waterford*, pp.177-9.

CHAPTER 7 – THE LAST BATTLES

1. *Voice of Labour*, 15 September 1923.

2. Glascott Symes, 'Sir John Keane and Cappoquin House during the turbulent times', *Decies*, 73 (2017), pp 105–18.

3. UCDA, Mulcahy papers, P7/B/321–22.

4. Pat McCarthy, *The Irish Revolution, 1912–23:Waterford* (Dublin, 2015), p. 118.
5. *Munster Express*, 10 February 1923.
6. SIPTU archives, Dublin, letters from Foran, 5, 11 April 1923.
7. Ibid., letters from Foran, 5, 11 April 1923; letter from J. Foley, 9 April 1923; Head Office memorandum, 16 May 1923; letter from Baird, 25 March 1923.
8. SIPTU archives, letter from Baird, 16 April 1923.
9. Ibid., 13 May 1923.
10. *Munster Express*, 19–26 May 1923.
11. A Head Office memorandum in SIPTU archives, dated 11 October 1923, stated the WFA final offer for outdoor workers in summertime to be 28s.6d. However, the sum of 30s. is reported in the *Munster Express*, 19 May 1923, and cited by R.A. Kelly in the *Munster Express*, 26 May 1923. Keane's remark is cited in the *Freeman's Journal*, 9 June 1923.
12. NLI, ITGWU Ms 27061, report on strikes, 24 April 1923.
13. SIPTU archives, Dublin, Head Office memorandum, 11 October 1923; *Munster Express*, 26 May, 2 June 1923. For the number of strikers and parishes involved see the *Voice of Labour*, 2 June, 8 August 1923.
14. SIPTU archives, letters from Baird, 12 and 14 June 1923.
15. *Munster Express*, 5 May 1923. On Larkin see Emmet O'Connor, *Big Jim Larkin: Hero or Wrecker?* (Dublin, 2015), pp 216–19.
16. *Munster Express*, 19–26 May 1923.
17. Ibid., 2 June 1923.
18. NLI, ITGWU papers, Ms 27062, correspondence with branches, June-July 1923, Waterford branch to Head Office, 14 June 1923, telegram, 15 June 1923.
19. Emmet O'Connor, *A Labour History of Waterford* (Waterford, 1989), plate 14; *Freeman's Journal*, 8 June 1923.
20. *Freeman's Journal*, 8 June 1923.
21. National Archives, Dublin, Dáil Éireann papers, cabinet papers, S 3110.
22. ITUC, *Annual Report*, 1920, p. 137, 1923, pp 20, 52.
23. *Irish Independent*, 26 June 1923; William O'Brien, *Forth the Banners Go: Reminiscences of William O'Brien as Told to Edward MacLysaght, D.Litt* (Dublin, 1969), p. 113.
24. *Freeman's Journal*, 19 June 1923.
25. O'Connor, *A Labour History of Waterford*, plate 14.
26. *Irish Independent*, 15 June 1923.
27. McAuliffe's report on the dispute is in NA, Dáil Éireann papers, cabinet papers, S 3110.
28. Emmet O'Connor, *A Labour History of Ireland, 1824–2000* (Dublin, 2011), p. 126.
29. SIPTU archives, Baird to Foran, 3 August 1923, and reply, 17 August 1923.
30. NLI, William O'Brien papers, Ms 15705(11); *Munster Express*, 28 June 1919; *Cork Examiner*, 10 March 1923.
31. The figure of 20,000 is based on newspaper reports. A similar estimate is found in UCDA, Mulcahy papers, P7/B/415. Official statistics understate the level of unrest.
32. *Irish Times*, 25 August 1923.
33. Cited in the *Munster Express*, 25 August 1923.
34. Dáil Éireann debates, vol.5, 432–3, 31 October 1923.
35. *Munster Express*, 1 September 1923.
36. *Manchester Evening News*, 30 August 1923.
37. *Munster Express*, 1 September 1923.
38. *Voice of Labour*, 15 September 1923.
39. *Freeman's Journal*, 2 June 1923; Dáil Éireann Debates, vol. 3, 1409–12, 31

May 1923; https://www.theirishstory.com/2015/10/15/rough-and-ready-work-the-special-infantry-corps, accessed 15 July 2021.
40. *Voice of Labour*, 15 September to 20 October 1923. Dáil Éireann Debates, vol.5, 432–33, 31 October 1923.
41. *Freeman's Journal*, 7, 26 September 1923; *Irish Independent*, 26 September 1923; *Liberator*, 8 September 1923; *Voice of Labour*, 15–22 September 1923; SIPTU archives, correspondence from Dunne, 12 September 1923; Dáil Éireann debates, 25 September 1923, vol.5, no.3.
42. *Waterford News*, 19 October 1923.
43. *Voice of Labour*, 3 November 1923.
44. *Leinster Leader*, 27 October 1923. I am obliged to Terry Dunne for this reference.
45. *Voice of Labour*, 15 September 1923; *Workers' Republic*, 29 September 1923; *Irish Worker*, 6 October 1923. Normal service in the *Irish Worker* resumed on 17 May 1924 when it disparaged the ITGWU's 'Lagansiders', implying that Baird and the Belfast Labour Party were associated with misappropriation of White Cross funds. The aspersions were typical of Larkin at this time.
46. *Irish Independent*, 21 September 1923; *Irish Times*, 29 September 1923.
47. *Freeman's Journal*, 13 October 1923; *Belfast News-Letter*, 20 October 1923; *Voice of Labour*, 20–27 October 1923; *Waterford News*, 7 December 1923; Dáil Éireann debates, 12 October 1923, vol.5, no.7.
48. UCDA, FitzGerald papers, O'Higgins to Mulcahy, 26 October 1923, P80/729(2-), cited in John Regan, *The Irish Counter-Revolution, 1921–1936: Treatyite Politics and Settlement in Independent Ireland* (Dublin, 1999), p. 177.
49. *Waterford News*, 10 November 1923.
50. *Freeman's Journal*, 23 November 1923; *Waterford News*, 7 December 1923.
51. Francis Devine, 'The Irish Transport and General Workers' Union in Waterford, 1918–1930', *Decies*, 74 (2018), pp 125–6.
52. SIPTU archives, Dublin, Head Office memoranda, 11 October, 16 October, 20 December 1923.
53. O'Brien, *Forth the Banners Go*, pp 113–14.

EPILOGUE – FROM THE BLACK SQUAD TO THE BLACK LEGEND

1. Marilyn Silverman, *An Irish Working Class: Explorations in Political Economy and Hegemony, 1800-1950* (Toronto, 2001), pp.265-7; *Kilkenny Journal*, 3 May 1924. *Kilkenny People*, 3 May 1924.
2. *Voice of Labour*, 12-26 January, 15 March, 10 May 1924.
3. NLI, ITGWU papers, Ms 27065, head office circular, 7 June 1924.
4. *Belfast News-Letter*, 8 January 1924.
5. Seanad Éireann debates, 14 December 1925, vol.6, no.3.
6. William O'Brien, *Forth the Banners Go: Reminiscences of William O'Brien as Told to Edward MacLysaght, D.Litt* (Dublin, 1969), p.114.
7. Dan O'Donnell, *Nora Baird, MBE (1900-1991)* (Brisbane, 1992), p.8.
8. Australian census, 1934. The census listed him as living in 234 Grey Street, South Brisbane. Frances's occupation in all Australian censuses was given as 'home duties'.
9. State of Queensland Death Certificate, no.B19941; *Brisbane Telegraph, Courier Mail*, 8 December 1948; *Belfast Telegraph*, 1 January 1949; *Northern Whig*, 3 January 1949; *Waterford Evening News*, 4 January 1949; *Munster Express*, 7 January 1949; *Waterford Standard*, 8 January 1949, NLI, William O'Brien papers, diary, Ms 16276.
10. *Brisbane Courier*, 6 May 1930; for the wider history see Raymond Evans and Carole Ferrier (ed), *Radical Brisbane: An Unruly History* (Carlton North, Victoria, 2004).

Bibliography

Private papers

Edward Carson, PRONI, D1507/A/30/12
Joseph Cunningham, PRONI, D1288/1A
Desmond FitzGerald, UCDA, P80/729(2-3)
John French, Imperial War Museum, 75/46/12
Richard Mulcahy, UCDA, P7/B/321-22, P7/B/415
Art Ó Briain, NLI, 8457/11, 8460/17
William O'Brien, NLI, 15705(11), 16276

Public records

British Parliamentary Papers
Royal Commission on Labour, Volume III, C.6894.X (1893)
Report to the Secretary of State for the Home Department on Accidents Occurring in Shipbuilding Yards, Cd.7046.LX (1913)
Report of the Proceedings of the Irish Convention, Cd.9019 (1918)

Derry City Council Archives
Letter book no. 50

General Register Office of Northern Ireland
Birth certificate, online

Irish Labour History Society Archive
ITUC national executive, minutes, 7 February1919

Modern Records Centre, University of Warwick
Amalgamated Society of Woodworkers, correspondence, 20, 26 October 1920, 78/ASW/3/1/21
BTUC, *Annual Reports*, 1920-1, online
United Society of Boilermakers and Iron and Steel Shipbuilders, *Monthly Reports*, 1918-19, Mss 192/BM/4/1/46

National Archives, Dublin
Census of Ireland, 1901, 1911, online
Dáil Éireann papers, DE 2/89, DE 2/110, DE 2/353, S 3110
ITUC, *Annual Reports*, 1902-3, 1911, 1913, 1918-21, online

National Archives, London
Dublin Castle records, CO 904/203/5
RIC, Crime Special Branch, CO 904/158/5
RIC Inspector General's monthly confidential reports, 1919, CO 904/108

Security service, personal files, KV 2/614

National Library
ITGWU papers, 27041, 27058, 27061, 27062, 27065

Public Record Office of Northern Ireland
Belfast trades council, minutes, 1888-1906, MIC 193/1
Belfast Corporation papers, LA/7/1/CA/2
UULA papers, minute book, 1917-23, D1327/11/4/1

Working Class Movement Library
NSFU, Annual Reports, 1918-22
United Society of Boilermakers and Iron and Steel Shipbuilders, *Monthly Reports*,
    1899-1921

Private reports

American Commission on Conditions in Ireland, *Interim Report* (New York, 1921)
Report of the American Committee for Relief in Ireland (New York, 1922)
Report of the Irish White Cross (New York, 1922)
British Labour Party, *Report of the Labour Commission to Ireland* (London, 1921)

Newspapers and journals

Belfast Evening Telegraph, 1903, 1906-7, 1911-12, 1918
Belfast Labour Chronicle, 1904-6
Belfast News-Letter, 1906, 1914, 1918-24
Belfast Telegraph, 1918, 1920-1, 1949
Birmingham Gazette, 1920
Brisbane Courier, 1930
Brisbane Telegraph, 1948
Church of Ireland Gazette, 1920-1
Communist, 1921
Cork Examiner, 1922-3
Courier Mail, 1948
Daily Herald, 1913, 1921
Derry Journal, 1919-22
Donegal News, 1922
Evening Echo, 1922
Evening Herald, 1922
Evening Telegraph, 1919-20
Freeman's Journal, 1922-3
Irish Citizen, 1915, 1920
Irish Freedom, 1939
Irish Independent, 1919-23
Irish News, 1903, 1905, 1907, 1918, 1920-1
Irishman, 1928
Irish Times, 1920-3
Irish Times Weekly, 1910
Irish Worker, 1923-4
Kilkenny Journal, 1924
Kilkenny People, 1922, 1924

Labour Leader, 1917
Liberator, 1923
Liverpool Echo, 1907
Manchester Evening News, 1923
Munster Express, 1919, 1923, 1949
NorthernWhig, 1884, 1905, 1907, 1912, 1914, 1917-19, 1921, 1949
Peasant, later the *Nation and Irish Ireland*, 1909-10
Railway Review, 1920
Rechabite, 1908
Ulster Herald, 1920
Voice of Labour, 1918-19, 1922-4
Watchword of Labour, 24 January 1920
Waterford Evening News, 1949
Waterford News, 1923
Waterford Standard, 8 January 1949
Westminster Gazette, 1920-1
Workers' Bulletin, 1919
Workers' Republic, 1922-3

Books and articles

Anonymous, *Tales of the RIC* (Edinburgh and London, 1921)
Barritt, Denis P. and Charles F. Carter, *The Northern Ireland Problem: A Study in Group Relations* (Oxford, 1962)
Bell, Geoffrey, *Hesitant Comrades: The Irish Revolution and the British Labour Movement* (London, 2016)
Black, Boyd, 'Reassessing Irish industrial relations and labour history: The north-east of Ireland up to 1921', *Historical Studies in Industrial Relations* XIV (autumn, 2002), p.82
Boyd, Andrew, *Fermenting Elements: The Labour Colleges in Ireland, 1924–1964* (Belfast, 1999)
Boyle, J.W., 'The Belfast Protestant Association and the Independent Orange Order, 1901–10', *Irish Historical Studies*, xiii, 60 (1962)
——, *The Irish Labor Movement in the Nineteenth Century* (Washington DC, 1988)
Clarkson, J.D., *Labour and Nationalism in Ireland* (NewYork, 1925)
Clarkson, L.A., 'Population change and urbanization, 1821–1911', in Liam Kennedy and Philip Ollerenshaw (eds), *An Economic History of Ulster, 1820–1939* (Manchester, 1985)
Coates, Ken and Tony Topham, *The History of the Transport and General Workers' Union, Volume 1, The Making of the Transport and General Workers' Union: The Emergence of the Labour Movement, 1870–1922, Part II, 1912–1922: From Federation to Amalgamation* (Oxford, 1991)
Coe, W.E., *The Engineering Industry of the North of Ireland* (Belfast, 1969)
Connolly, James, 'Belfast and its problems', in *CollectedWorks*, vol.1 (Dublin, 1987)
Cullen, L.M., *An Economic History of Ireland Since 1660* (London, 1987)
Cradden, Terry, 'Trade unionism, social justice, and religious discrimination in Northern Ireland', *Industrial and Labor Relations Review*, 46:3 (1993)
Devine, Francis, *Organising History: A Centenary of SIPTU, 1909–2009* (Dublin, 2009)
——, 'The IrishTransport and GeneralWorkers' Union in Waterford, 1918–1930', *Decies*, 74 (2018)

Devlin, Paddy, *Yes We Have No Bananas: Outdoor Relief in Belfast, 1920–39* (Belfast, 1981)

Evans, Raymond and Carole Ferrier (ed), *Radical Brisbane: An Unruly History* (Carlton North, Victoria, 2004)

Farrell, Michael, *Northern Ireland: The Orange State* (London, 1976)

——, 'The establishment of the Ulster Special Constabulary', in Austen Morgan and Bob Purdie (eds), *Ireland: Divided Nation, Divided Class* (London, 1980)

Fitzpatrick, David, 'Strikes in Ireland, 1914–21', *Saothar*, 6 (1980)

Gaughan, J. Anthony, *Thomas Johnson, 1872–1963* (Dublin, 1980)

——, (ed), *Memoirs of Senator James G. Douglas (1887–1954): Concerned Citizen* (Dublin, 1998)

Grant, Adrian, *Derry: The Irish Revolution, 1912–23* (Dublin, 2018)

Gray, John, *City in Revolt: James Larkin and the Belfast Dock Strike of 1907* (Belfast, 1985)

Greaves, C. Desmond, *The Life and Times of James Connolly* (London, 1962)

——, *The Irish Transport and General Workers' Union: The Formative Years, 1909–23* (Dublin, 1982)

Greer, James and Graham Walker, 'Awkward Prods: Biographical studies of progressive Protestants and political allegiance in Northern Ireland', *Irish Political Studies*, 33:2 (2018)

Haire, Wilson John, 'The human history of a shipyard, 1–4', *Irish Political Review*, September-December (2020)

Hanna, Sandy, 'Yarns from the vineyard', *The Red Hand Magazine* (September 1920)

Henderson, MP, Arthur, *Nonconformity and Ireland* (London, 1921)

Hepburn, A.C., 'Work, class, and religion in Belfast, 1871–1911', *Irish Economic and Social History*, X (1983)

Higenbottam, S., *Amalgamated Society of Woodworkers: Our Society's History* (Manchester, 1939)

Hill, Myrtle, 'Labour lives, no.19: Margaret Taylor McCoubrey (1880–1956), *Saothar*, 44 (2019)

Hirst, Catherine, 'Politics, sectarianism, and the working class in nineteenth century Belfast', in Fintan Lane and Dónal Ó Drisceoil, *Politics and The Irish Working Class, 1830–1945* (London, 2005)

Hopkinson, Michael, 'The Craig-Collins Pacts of 1922: two attempted reforms of the Northern Ireland government', *Irish Historical Studies* 27:106 (November, 1990)

Hutt, Allen, *British Trade Unionism: A Short History* (London, 1975)

Hutchinson, Keith, *The Decline and Fall of British Capitalism* (London, 1951)

Independent Order of Rechabites, *Belfast Moveable Conference Souvenir Book* (1899)

Isles, K.S. and N. Cuthbert, *Economic Survey of Northern Ireland* (Belfast, 1957)

Johnson, D.S., 'The Belfast boycott, 1920–22', in J.M. Goldstrom and L.A. Clarkson (eds), *Irish Population, Economy, and Society: Essays in Honour of the Late K.H. Connell* (Oxford, 1981)

Kenna, G.B., *Facts and Figures of the Belfast Pogroms, 1920–22* (Dublin, 1922, 2nd edn, 1997)

Lacy, Brian, *Siege City: The Story of Derry and Londonderry* (Belfast, 1990)

Loughlin, Christopher J.V., *Labour and the Politics of Disloyalty in Belfast, 1921–39: The Moral Economy of Loyalty* (Cham, Switzerland, 2018)

Lynch, John, 'Technology, labour, and the growth of Belfast shipbuilding', *Saothar*, 24 (1999)

——, 'The Belfast shipyards and the industrial working class', in Francis Devine, Fintan Lane, and Niamh Puirséil (eds), *Essay in Irish Labour History: A Festschrift for Elizabeth and John W. Boyle* (Dublin, 2008)

Lynch, Robert, *The Partition of Ireland, 1918–1925* (Cambridge, 2019)

MacDiarmada, Mary, *Art O'Brien and Irish Nationalism in London, 1900–1925* (Dublin, 2020)

Maguire, W.A., *Belfast* (Keele, 1993)

Marsh, Arthur and Victoria Ryan, *The Seamen: A History of the National Union of Seamen* (Oxford, 1989)

McCabe, Anton, '"The stormy petrel of the Transport Workers": Peadar O'Donnell, trade unionist, 1917–1920 in Derry', *Saothar*, 19 (1994)

McCabe, Conor, 'The Irish Labour Party and the 1920 local elections', *Saothar*, 35 (2010)

McCarthy, Pat, *The Irish Revolution, 1912–23: Waterford* (Dublin, 2015)

Mecham, Mike, 'William Walker: Social activist and Belfast labourist', *Saothar*, 43 (2018)

——, *William Walker: Social Activist and Belfast Labourist, 1870–1918* (Dublin, 2019)

Meenan, James, *The Irish Economy Since 1922* (Liverpool, 1971)

Mitchell, Arthur, *Labour in Irish Politics, 1890–1930: The Irish Labour Movement in an Age of Revolution* (Dublin, 1974)

Morgan, Austen, *Labour and Partition: The Belfast Working Class, 1905–23* (London, 1991)

Morgan, Kevin, *Bolshevism, Syndicalism, and the General Strike: The Lost Internationalist World of A.A. Purcell* (London, 2013)

Morrissey, C., '"Rotten Protestants": Protestant home rulers and the Ulster Liberal Association, 1906–1918', *Historical Journal*, 61:3 (2018)

Morrissey, Thomas J., *William O'Brien, 1881–1968: Socialist, Republican, Dáil Deputy, Editor, and Trade Union Leader* (Dublin, 2007)

Mortimer, J.E., *History of the Boilermakers' Society* (London, 1973)

——, *A History of the Boilermakers' Society: Volume 2, 1906–1939* (London, 1982)

Moulton, Mo, *Ireland and the Irish in Interwar Britain* (Cambridge, 2014)

Munck, Ronnie, 'The formation of the working class in Belfast, 1788–1881, *Saothar*, 11 (1986)

Nevin, Donal, *James Connolly: A Full Life* (Dublin, 2005)

Norton, Christopher, 'Worker response to the 1920 shipyard expulsions: Solidarity or sectarianism?', *Études Irlandaises*, 21–1 (1996)

——, 'An earnest endeavour for peace? Unionist opinion and the Craig/Collins peace pact of 30 March 1922', *Etudes Irlandaises* 32:1 (2007)

O'Brien, William, *Forth the Banners Go: Reminiscences of William O'Brien as Told to Edward MacLysaght, D. Litt* (Dublin, 1969)

O'Connor, Emmet, *Syndicalism in Ireland, 1917–23* (Cork, 1988)

——, *A Labour History of Waterford* (Waterford, 1989)

——, 'Labour lives; Cathal O'Shannon', *Saothar*, 24 (1999)

——, '"Sentries of British imperialism"? The question of British based unions in Ireland', *Socialist History*, 29 (2006)

——, 'William Walker, Irish Labour, and 'Chinese slavery' in South Africa, 1904–6', *Irish Historical Studies*, xxxvii, 145 (May 2010)

——, *A Labour History of Ireland, 1824–2000* (Dublin, 2011)

——, *Derry labour in the Age of Agitation, 1889–1923, Volume 1: New Unionism and Old, 1889–1906* (Dublin, 2014)

——, *Big Jim Larkin: Hero or Wrecker?* (Dublin, 2015)

——, *Derry Labour in the Age of Agitation, 1889–1923: Volume 2, Larkinism and Syndicalism, 1907–23* (Dublin, 2016)

——, 'Persona non grata: Andrew Boyd, 1921–2011', Francis Devine and Kieran Jack McGinley (eds), *Left Lives: Volume 2* (Dublin, 2019)

O'Connor, Emmet and Trevor Parkhill (eds), *Loyalism and Labour: The Autobiography of Robert McElborough, 1884–1952* (Cork, 2002)

O'Connor Lysaght, D.R., 'Labour lives, no.7', *Saothar*, 30 (2005)

O'Donnell, Dan, *Nora Baird, MBE (1900–1991)* (Brisbane, 1992)

O'Neill, Terence, *The Autobiography of Terence O'Neill* (London, 1972)

Parkinson, Alan F., *Belfast's Unholy War: The Troubles of the 1920s* (Dublin, 2004)

——, *A Difficult Birth: The Early Years of Northern Ireland, 1920–25* ((Dublin, 2020)

Parr, Connal, 'Expelled from yard and tribe: the "Rotten Prods" of 1920 and their political legacies', *Studi Irlandesi: A Journal of Irish Studies*, 11 (2021)

Parr, Connal and Aaron Edwards, 'Breaking from the herd: The "Rotten Prod" tradition in Ulster labour history', *Essays in Honour of Joe Law* (Dublin, 2018)

Patterson, Henry, *Class Conflict and Sectarianism: The Protestant Working Class and the Belfast Labour Movement, 1868–1920* (Belfast, 1980)

——, 'Industrial labour and the labour movement, 1820–1914', in Liam Kennedy and Phillip Ollerenshaw, *An Economic History of Ulster, 1820–1939* (Manchester, 1985)

——, 'The Belfast shipyard expulsions of 1920', in Emmet O'Connor (ed), *Labour and Northern Ireland: Foundation and Development* (Belfast, 2019)

Pollard, Sidney and Paul Robertson, *The British Shipbuilding Industry, 1870–1914* (Cambridge, Ma, 1979)

Purdie, Bob, 'Trade and Ulster Unionist: Senator Joseph Cunningham', *Labour History News* 4 (1988)

Radford, Mark, *The Policing of Belfast 1870–1914* (London, 2015)

Regan, John M., *The Irish Counter-Revolution, 1921–1936: Treatyite Politics and Settlement in Independent Ireland* (Dublin, 1999)

Reid, Alastair, 'Skilled workers in the shipbuilding industry, 1880–1920: A labour aristocracy?', in Austen Morgan and Bob Purdie (eds), *Ireland: Divided Nation, Divided Class* (London, 1980)

Silverman, Marilyn, *An Irish Working Class: Explorations in Political Economy and Hegemony, 1800–1950* (Toronto, 2001)

Smylie, Patrick. 'A cautionary antecedent: The Belfast career of John Bruce Wallace', in Seán Byers (ed), *William Walker, 1870–1918: Belfast Labour Unionist Centenary Essays* (Dublin, 2018)

Symes, Glascott, 'Sir John Keane and Cappoquin House during the turbulent times', *Decies*, 73 (2017)

Sweeney, Pat, *Liffey Ships and Shipbuilding* (Cork, 2010)

Walker, Graham, *The Politics of Frustration: Harry Midgley and the Failure of Labour in Northern Ireland* (Manchester, 1985)

Wilson, Alec, *PR Urban Elections in Ulster, 1920* (London, 1972)

Wrigley, C.J., *1919: The Critical Year* (Loughborough, 2019)

Yeates, Pádraig, 'Craft workers during the Irish revolution, 1919–22', *Saothar*, 33 (2008)

——, 'The men 'going into the Convention…did not own their own souls': The Labour movement and the Irish Convention', *Saothar*, 45 (2020)

Dissertations

Collins, Peter Gerard, 'Belfast trades council, 1881–1921' (D.Phil, University of Ulster, 1988)
Harding, Keith, 'The Irish issue in the British labour movement, 1900–1922' (PhD, University of Essex, 1983)
Morgan, Austen, 'Politics, the labour movement and the working class in Belfast, 1905–23' (PhD, Queen's University, Belfast, 1978)
Smylie, Patrick, "Socialism of the mild type': the political thought and action of Reverend J. Bruce Wallace, and radical politics in Belfast, 1884–91' (MA, Queen's University, Belfast, 2010)

e-sources/online

Australian census, 1934
State of Queensland Death Certificate, no.B19941
Rast, Michael C., "The mad dance of death': The Ulster Protestant Association in Belfast, 1921–22', https://www.theirishstory.com/2016/02/15/the-mad-dance-of-death-the-ulster-protestant-association-in-belfast-1921-22/#.YR_t7Y5KiUk, accessed 16 August 2021
https://www.theirishstory.com/2015/10/15/rough-and-ready-work-the-special-infantry-corps, accessed 15 July 2021
https://www.ictu.ie/blog/2019/11/12/the-belfast-pogrom-extract-from-labourgender-and-c/, accessed 15 September 2020.
Dáil Éireann debates, 1923
Seanad Éireann debates, 1925
https://www.oireachtas.ie/en/debates/debate/dail/1920-08-06/, accessed 3 October 2020

Index

Adair, Henry 65
Adams, Alex 61, 63
Addis, J. 35
Agricultural Wages Board xiv
agricultural workers xiii–xiv, 80
    and ITGWU 83–9
    strike 83–95
    wages 83–5
agriculture xiii–xiv
Amalgamated Cabinetmakers,
    Carpenters, and Joiners (ASCJ)
    8, 15, 26, 48, 50, 54–5, 67
Amalgamated Engineering Union
    (AEU) 15, 48, 55
Amalgamated Marine Workers'
    Union 65
Amalgamated Society of Engineers
    (ASE) xiii, 5, 8, 15, 19, 26, 28
    militancy 21
Amalgamated Society of
    Woodworkers 55, 67, 69–71
Amalgamated Transport and General
    Workers' Union 4, 81
amalgamated unions xii, xv, 54, 57,
    66–7, 69, 78
American Commission on
    Conditions in Ireland 47
American Committee for Relief in
    Ireland (Amcomri) 47
Ancient Order of Hibernians 16, 47,
    51
Andrews, J.M. 74
Anglo-Irish Treaty 72, 75, 78, 90
anti-conscription campaign 15, 26
Anti-German Union 34
apprenticeships 3, 7
Armagh, County 74
arson 46–7, 81, 84, 93–4

Bagenalstown, Co. Carlow 79
Baird, Eileen 6, 13
Baird, Frances Lavina (née Miller) 6,
    79, 97

Baird, Geneve 6, 76
Baird, George (Sr) 1
Baird, George (Jr) 6
Baird, James
    arrest 93–4
    articles and letters 9, 24, 30, 49,
        72, 75–6, 87, 89
    and BEW 67–71
    death 97
    early life 1
    and EWRC 48, 56–7
    family 6, 14, 79
    and Harland and Wolff xii, 2–3,
        12–13
    hunger strike 94
    ill-health 72, 94
    marriage 6
    political activity: Belfast
        Corporation 31, 33–5,
        39, 50–1, 60, 76; Belfast
        Labour 56; Belfast
        trades council 9; contests
        elections 59–64, 88–9,
        91–2
    religion xii, 1, 6–7, 42, 66
    speeches 22–3, 35–6, 39, 57–8,
        59, 66–73, 81–2, 91, 95, 96
    travels to Australia 97
    union activities: Boilermakers'
        Society 13–14, 21–3,
        30; GSC 23–4; ITGWU
        59, 66, 77–; NSFU 59,
        64–6; organiser, Waterford
        78–82, 83–95
    views: Anglo-Irish treaty 72;
        BTUC 67–8; Collins
        75; education 29; FEST
        30; expulsions 67–71;
        globalisation 10–11; Home
        Rule 9–10, 29; housing 37,
        40; land nationalisation
        11, 13, 87; monarchy
        68–9; partition 59–60, 66;

republicanism 43, 59, 64, 98; socialism 1, 9–10, 21, 42, 60, 68, 98; syndicalism 30, 83; trade unionism 24
visits Dublin 57–8, 73
visits London 71–2
and the *Voice of Labour* 9, 28–30, 87–8
Baird, John 1
Baird, Helene 6, 14, 97
Baird, Kathleen 6
Baird, Margaret (née Wright) 1
Baird, Nora xii, 6, 14, 76, 79, 97–8
Ballymacarrett, Belfast 3, 13–14, 30, 45, 47, 79
Barnes, Dermot 64
Barritt, Denis P. 15
Beard, John 53, 70–1
Beattie, Jack 65
Behan (Miller), Jane 6
Belfast 29 *see also* by-elections; trades councils
  constituencies 7, 12–13, 51
  economic growth 1–2
  living conditions 5–7
  riots 15
  violence in 41–58
Belfast Boycott 53, 55–6, 72–3
Belfast City Council 35
Belfast City Hall 23, 25, 36, 60, 64, 70, 76
Belfast Corporation 9, 31–40, 44, 50, 60–1, 76, 81, 96
Belfast Evening Star 10
Belfast Evening Telegraph 11
Belfast Expelled Workers (BEW) 67–8, 72–5
Belfast Labour Chronicle 12
Belfast Labour Party 19, 31–5, 37, 39, 60–1, 70, 73
Belfast News-Letter 14, 22–3, 25–6, 32, 36, 40, 45, 61–2, 64, 96
Belfast Protestant Association 12, 41, 43
Belfast Radical Association 10
Belfast Socialist Society 9
Belfast Telegraph 42, 44, 69
Belfast Weekly Star 10
Bell, James 30
Bennett, James H. 65
'Black Friday' 77
black squad xii, 3, 14, 27, 29, 96

boilermakers 2, 4–5
Boilermakers' Society (Society of Friendly Boilermakers, United Friendly Boiler Makers' Society) xiii, 5, 7–9, 11, 13, 18, 21–2, 28, 42, 44, 57, 63
  Good Samaritan Lodge xiii
  Monthly Review 49
  relief fund 49
Bolshevik revolution 14, 24
Bolshevism 42, 63, 88
Boundary Commission 74
Boyd, Alex 12–13, 34
Boyd, Andrew 15
Boyd, Robert 61–2
Bradley, Sam 34, 68–9
Breen, Dan 90
Brennock, Michael 92
Brisbane, Australia 97–8
British Empire Union 34, 43, 61
British Labour Party 11, 15, 17–19, 43, 49, 53–4
British Seafarers' Union 65
British Socialist Party 43
British Trades Union Congress (BTUC) 35, 40, 51–5, 67–8
British Workers' League 43
Brugha, Caitlín 90, 92
Brugha, Cathal 90
Butler, Jack 86, 89, 92, 94
by-elections
  1902: Belfast South 7
  1905: Belfast North 12
  1907: Belfast 70; Liverpool Kirkdale 13
Byrne, Daniel 90
Campbell, D.R. 16, 35
Campbell, Davy 18, 33, 36–7, 50, 68
Campbell, Hugh 37
Carlow, County xii, 80–1
Carney, Winifred 28
Carruthers, W.H. 51
Carson, Sir Edward 17, 22, 34, 41, 43–5, 55, 67
Carter, Charles F. 15
Cassidy, Thomas 27
Castledawson, County Derry 16
Catholic Church 24, 45, 56
Catholics xii, xiv–xv, 15–17, 33, 38, 41–2, 45, 74
  victimisation of 42–58, 75
caulkers 2–3, 7

Church of Ireland xiv, 6
Church of Ireland Gazette 25, 58, 63
Churchill, Winston 75
Citizen Army xiii, 95
Civil War 78, 80, 84, 90
Clark, George 'Orange' 13
Clark, Joseph T. 51
class war 24, 67
Clyde Workers' Committee 22
Clydeside 5, 14, 21–2, 26
Collins, Michael 57, 72–5
Committee of Production 20
communism 14
Communist 41
Communist International 25
Communist Party 79
Communist Party of Great Britain
    14, 71
Comrades of the Great War 43
Congregational Church 10
Connolly, James xiii, 4–6, 17–18, 59,
    78, 88
Connolly, Joe 38
Conservative Party xiv–xv, 11–13,
    17–18, 21
Conservative Associations 15
Convery, Fr P. 51
Coombe, Barbour, Fairbairn and
    Lawson 54
co-operatives 30
Cork Employers' Federation 91
Cosgrave, W.T. 80, 84
craft unions xiii, 7–8, 26, 30, 57
craftsmen *see* skilled workers
Craig, Sir James 61–2, 64, 72–5
Craig–Collins pacts 72–5
Cumann na nGaedheal 84, 92
Cunningham, Joseph 16
Custom House, Belfast 15, 36

Dáil Éireann 38, 46–7, 55–6, 66, 72,
    75, 90–2
Daily Herald 29, 39, 56–7, 59, 71
Davidson & Company 54
Davison, William 12
Dawson Bates, Sir Richard 17, 25–6,
    32, 74
de Blaghd, Earnán 56
de Valera, Éamon 47, 61, 66, 80
Dee, Éamonn 90
Derry City xiv, 27, 35, 42, 66, 74, 77
    see also trades councils

rioting in 41
unions in 66
Derry Corporation 35
Derry Workers' Education
    Committee 38–9
Devlin, Joe 13, 56, 60, 75
Dixon, Sir Daniel ('Dodger Dan')
    9, 12
dock strikes
    1907 34
    1923 91
Doherty, John 51
Donald, Thompson 16
Donaldson, George 34–5
Down, County 74
Dublin City Hall 73
Dungarvan Observer 90
Dutton, C.B. 72–3

Easter Rising xiii, 79
education 3, 10, 29
Edwards, Aaron xiv
elections *see* by-elections; general
    elections; local elections;
    Northern Ireland elections
Electrical Trades Union 26, 48
Employers' Liability Act 5
engineering, marine 2
Engineering Employers' Federation
    21–2
Evening Telegraph 58
evictions 47, 50
Expelled Workers' Committee 16, 51
Expelled Workers' Relief Committee
    (EWRC) 46, 48, 51–3, 55, 57,
    69
expulsions/expelled workers 16,
    42–58, 60, 71–2, 74–5 *see
    also* Belfast Expelled Workers
    (BEW)

Factory Acts 5
Fair Employment Act 15
farm workers *see* agricultural workers
Farmers' Party 84, 90–2
Federation of Engineering and
    Shipbuilding Trades (FEST) 8,
    16, 21–2, 27–8, 48, 55, 70
Fegan, Joseph 51
Fermanagh, County 74
Finnegan, P. 51
First World War 14, 21, 37

impact in Ireland xiii, 20
Fitzgerald, Nicholas 90
Flavin, Garret 92
Foran, Thomas 77–9, 83–6, 88–9, 95
Free Church 7
Free State xv, 74, 80, 83–4, 87, 90, 93
Free State army 80, 87
Freeland, James 19, 21, 48
freemasons 15
French, Sir John 28
friendly societies 7
Friendly Society of Operative Iron
    Moulders 22

gasworks strike 81–2
general elections 75
    1906 12–13
    1918 18–19, 22, 28, 31, 65
    1922 88–90
    1923 80, 89–92, 98
General, Municipal and
    Boilermakers' Union 15
general strike committee (GSC)
    23–8, 30
George, Harrison 94
George, Henry 10
Getgood, Bob 4
Gladstone, William xiv
Glasgow 6, 22, 24–5, 26–8 *see also*
    Clydeside
globalisation 10–11
Gordon, Dawson 32, 35
Government of Ireland Act 40, 42, 61
Grant, William (Billy) 16, 26
Greenspon, Simon Wolfe 24–5, 36–7,
    48, 56–7, 66–7, 74–5
Greenwood, Sir Hamar 44–5, 56
Greer, James xiv

Hacket Pain, Sir William 45
Haire, Wilson John xii
Hanna, Revd ('Roaring') Hugh 10
Hanna, John 13, 18
Hanna, John Alexander 48–50, 52,
    60–3, 66–71, 73
Hardie, Keir 12, 47
Harland and Wolff xii, 1–2, 15, 16,
    44, 48–50, 54
    apprenticeships 3
    hierarchy 2–3
    wages 3–4
Harris, Joseph 9

Haslett, Sam 30, 60, 67, 73
Hassan, Fr James (G.B. Kenna) xi, 48
Hedley, Bella Sarah 25
Hedley (O'Hagan), Jack 'Shanghai'
    25–6
Henderson, Arthur 7, 54
Heron, Archie 65
Hill, John 13, 49, 53–4, 57, 69–70
Home Rule xiv–xv, 10, 12, 17–19, 32,
    45, 65
    crises 15, 42, 59
    opposition to 29
housing 5, 10, 32, 37
Houston, Denis 27, 33, 35, 37, 51,
    80, 93
Hughes, Séamus 78
hunger strikes 37, 94

Independent Labour Party (ILP) 11,
    13, 17–19, 28, 33, 35–6, 47,
    60–1, 65, 67
Independent Labour Party (of
    Ireland) 17
Independent Unionists 33
industrial accidents 4–5
International Labour Organisation 24
International Transport Workers'
    Federation 65
Insurance acts 77
Irish Bulletin 32
Irish Convention 14, 18
Irish Dominion League 56
Irish Engineering, Electric,
    Shipbuilding, and Foundry
    Trade Union 57
Irish Farmers' Union (IFU) 83–4, 88
Irish Labour Party 19, 53, 75, 77, 88,
    89–91
Irish Labour Press 28
Irish Land Restoration Society 10
Irish Linenlappers' and Warehouse
    Workers' Union 61, 66
Irish Nationalist Veterans' Association
    49
Irish News 61
Irish Republican Army (IRA) 41–2,
    47, 75, 78, 80, 84
    prisoners 90, 94
Irish Self-Determination League
    51, 56, 72 *see also* self-
    determination
Irish Times 32, 45, 91

Irish Trades Union Congress (ITUC)
8, 15, 18, 26–8, 30, 31–2, 52–4,
65, 67, 75, 77–9
Parliamentary Committee 16
Irish Transport and General Workers'
Union (ITGWU) (One Big
Union (OBU)) xiii–xiv, 27–8,
30, 32, 51, 59, 65–6, 77–9, 85,
89, 93–5 *see also* agricultural
workers
Larkin split 86–7
marine section 66
in Waterford 79–82, 87–8
Irish Worker 94
iron caulkers 2–3
Islandmen 15, 21, 62 *see also*
shipyards

Jackson, T.A. 71
James Connolly College 39
Johnson, Tom 52–4, 67, 73
Johnston, Thomas 9
Joint Vigilance Committee 55 *see also*
vigilance committees
J.W. Hey 71

Keane, Sir John 83–4
Keane, Richard 92
Keating, Peter 31, 71–3
Kelly, R.A. 86
Kenna, G.B. (Fr James Hassan) xi, 48
Kennedy, J.A. 35
Kennedy, T. 35
Kenny, Patrick 1, 96–7
Kilkenny, County xii, 78–81
Kilkenny gaol 93–4
Kilkenny infirmary 94
Kyle, Sam 19, 35, 37, 60

Labour, Department of 56
Labour Board 57
Labour movement xiv–xv, 8, 51–7,
67, 80, 87, 93
Australian 98
Belfast 11
British 7, 11–12
Labour Party *see* Belfast Labour
Party; British Labour Party;
Independent Labour Party
(ILP); Irish Labour Party;
Northern Ireland Labour Party

Labour Representation Committee
(LRC) 11–12, 18, 22
labour Unionism 15–17, 32, 43
land ownership xiv, 11, 13, 87–8
Larkin, James xi, xiii, 34, 78, 84,
86–7, 90, 97
Lawther, J.S. 35
Legion of Irish Ex-Servicemen 90
Lemass, Noel 93
Leo XIII, Pope 27
Liberal Party xiv, 7, 56
Liberty Hall, Dublin xiii, 59, 77–8,
86, 91
local elections
1920 31–3, 44
1924 96
Local Government (Ireland) Act
(1919) 31
lockout funds 48
lockouts xiii, 26, 88
Logue, Cardinal Michael 29
Logue, William 28–9
London Connolly Club 7
Lorimer, William 19, 30
Lowe, F. 53, 70
loyalism xii, 15–16, 34, 37–9, 42–3,
47–50, 57–8, 61–3, 69, 71, 74
Lundon, Thomas 18
Lynn, Robert 24

McAuliffe, M.B. 85–6, 88–9
McCarron, James 18
McClung, Robert 10
McCoubrey, Margaret 18
McCoy, Bernard 64
McCullagh, Sir Crawford 64
McDevitt, Danny 73
McDonagh, Joseph 56
MacDonald, James Ramsay 12–13,
17
McElborough, Robert 34
McGrath, Joseph 73–4
McGuffin, Sam 19
McInnes, Edward 11
McKay, Alex 62
McKay, Charles 18
McKeag, J.S.L. 35
Mackie's 54
McLaughlin and Harvey 54
McMahon, Owen 75
McMahon massacre 75–6
McMordie, Julia 64

McMullen, William 67
MacNeill, Eoin 38–9
McNulty, Bill 77
Macpherson, Ian 23
McRandall, Daniel 51
MacRory, Bishop Joseph 41
MacSwiney, Terence 56
Manchester Evening News 91
Mandeville, John 90
Mann, Tom 71
Markievicz, Constance 56–7
marriage, interdenominational 6
May Day 39–40, 66, 98
Metcalfe, Joe 81
Midgley, Harry 60–3, 66
Milan, John 26, 30, 48
Miller, Frances *see* Baird, Frances
    Lavina
Miller, Jane (née Behan) 6, 13
Miller, Robert 6, 13
Miners' Federation 77
Moles, Thomas 64
Morel, E.D. 39
Morgan, Austen 24, 44–5
Morning News 24
Morrissey, C. xiv
Mulcahy, Richard 94
Munster Express 90
Murphy, John 18
Musgrave's 54

National Amalgamated Union of
    Labour (NAUL) 4, 11, 18, 33,
    68, 71
National Amalgamated Union of Life
    Assurance Workers 68
National Democratic and Labour
    Party 43
National Maritime Board 65
National Sailors' and Firemen's
    Union (NSFU) 59, 64–6, 77
National Transport Workers'
    Federation 65, 77
National Union of Railwaymen 49,
    77
National Union of Ships' Stewards,
    Cooks, Bakers and Butchers 65
National Volunteers 47
nationalism xiv–xv, 9, 17, 22, 26–7,
    37, 47, 58
Nationalists 15, 22, 31–7, 48, 50, 64
non-conformism xiv, 7

Northern Democrat 37–8
Northern Ireland elections (1921)
    60–4
Northern Ireland Labour Party 61
Northern Ireland parliament 59
Northern Whig 24, 26, 50, 61–2, 72

O'Brien, Art 72
O'Brien, William 77–9, 83–4, 86–7,
    93, 95, 97
O'Donnell, Peadar 39, 66, 77
O'Donoghue 52
O'Farrell, J.T. 52, 97
O'Hagan (Hedley), Jack 25–6
O'Higgins, Kevin 77, 81, 93–4
Olde Castle Restaurant, Belfast
    11–12
O'Meagher, Charles 25
One Big Union (OBU) *see* Irish
    Transport and General
    Workers' Union (ITGWU)
O'Neill, Terence 26
Orange Order 10, 26, 34, 43, 63
O'Shannon, Cathal 28–9
O'Sullivan, E.J. 97

Parr, Connal xiv
partition 17–18, 63
    opposition to 18, 40, 59, 60,
    65–6
Patterson, William Forbes 37–9, 44–5
Peace With Ireland Council 56
Peasant 29
Phelan, Nicholas 89–90
Pirrie, Lord 50
Plunkett, Horace 14
Plymouth Brethren 60, 63
Pollitt, Harry 14
Pollock, Hugh MacDowell 64
Porter, Samuel 19, 40, 65
Presbyterianism xiv, 6–7, 16, 48, 63
proportional representation 31–3, 60
Proportional Representation Society
    of Ireland 33
Protestants xii, xiv–xv, 1, 6, 10–12,
    14, 16, 19, 28, 33–4, 37, 39,
    41–8, 50, 52, 57–8, 61–3, 72,
    84 *see also* Belfast Protestant
    Association; Ulster Protestant
    Association
Provision of School Meals Act 60
Provisional Government xi, 73, 78

Public Safety (Emergency Powers)
  Act 93
Pugh, Arthur 53–4, 69–70
Purcell, A.A. (Alf) 53–5, 69–70

Queen's Island, Belfast 1, 3, 10, 25 *see also* Islandmen

Railway Clerks' Association 52
Railway Review 49
railwaymen 49
railways 20
Rechabites xii, 7
Red Hand Magazine 39
Redmond, John 16–17
Redmond, Revd John 45, 47
Redmond, William 37, 90, 92
republicanism xiv, 17–18, 32, 38, 45,
  47, 52, 56–7, 59, 66, 71, 80, 87,
  90–1, 93, 98
Rerum Novarum 27
Revolutionary Socialist Party of
  Ireland 25
Ridgway, Charlie 66
Right to Work Committee 9, 12
Robinson, Séamus 90
Royal Commission on Labour xiii,
  2–4
Royal Irish Constabulary (RIC) 16,
  28, 36, 41, 43
Ryan, Tommy 86
Ryan, W.P. 29

St Vincent de Paul 51
Saklatvala, Shapurji 71
Scott, Clarke 35, 56–7
Scottish Trades Union Congress 50
sectarianism 15–16
self-determination 40, 49, 53 *see also* Irish Self-Determination
  League
Shackleton, David 7
Shannon Electrification Scheme 96
shipyards 2–5, 10 *see also* expulsions/
  expelled workers; Harland and
  Wolff; Workman, Clark
  accidents 5
  earnings 20
  militancy 4, 21
  sectarianism 15
  unions 11
shop stewards 14, 20–2, 44

Sinn Féin 19, 22, 25–6, 28, 31–3, 38,
  41–2, 44–5, 49–51, 54–6, 58,
  61, 89–91
Sirocco Works 45, 54
skilled workers 3–5, 20–1
Sloan, Tom 7, 12–13
Smith, T.J. 16
Smyth, Gerald 41–2, 44–5, 55
Social Democratic Federation 11
socialism xiv, 10, 38–9, 41–3, 50–1,
  60–6
  opposition to 11, 17–18, 61
Socialist Party of Ireland 17, 28
Society of Friendly Boilermakers *see*
  Boilermakers
soviets 23, 81–2, 88
Special Infantry Corps 84, 93
spirit groceries 45–7
Stewart, Alexander 51
strikes 26, 91 *see also* agricultural
  workers; dock strikes; gasworks
  strike; general strike committee
  (GSC)
  44 hours engineering strike xi,
    xv, 21–30
  on demarcation 4
  on expulsions 54–5
  Glasgow 26–8
  ITGWU 79
Swanzy, District Inspector 49
syndicalism xi, xiii, 24, 30, 69, 78,
  83, 98

Tales of the RIC 25
Thomas, J.H. 77–8, 89
Thomas, Leo 61–2
tillage orders xiii, 83
Times, The 24–5, 91, 93
Titanic 5
Tories *see* Conservative Party
trade unionism xii, 8–9, 21, 24–5,
  29, 38, 41, 47, 53, 58, 69, 72,
  88, 98 *see also* craft unions;
  shipyards
  agricultural 95
trades councils 31–2
  Belfast xiv, 6–9, 11–13, 15–18,
    26, 31
  Cork 18
  Derry 32, 35
  Dublin 18, 28

Trades Unionist Watch Committee 17
Travers 52
Treaty of Versailles 24
Turkington, James 43
Tyneside 5
Tyneside and National Labour Union 4
Tyrone, County 1, 74

Ulster Defence Association 95
Ulster Ex-Servicemen's Association 41, 43, 45, 61
Ulster Hall, Belfast 10, 16, 18, 21–2, 59, 61–2, 64–5
Ulster Herald 56
Ulster Imperial Guards 71
Ulster Protestant Association 43–4
Ulster Society for the Prevention of Cruelty to Animals 34
Ulster Socialist Party 18
Ulster Unionist Council 16, 53
Ulster Unionist Labour Association (UULA) 17, 19, 22, 26, 28, 32–5, 42, 44–5, 48, 57, 70–1, 74
Ulster Volunteer Force 45, 60, 66
Ulster Workers' Union 17, 43, 57, 71
unemployment 4, 9–10, 41–2, 49, 52, 61, 77, 81
Union of Democratic Control 56
Unionism xiv, 13, 15, 25–6, 38, 60–5, 67 *see also* labour Unionism
Unionist Party xv, 22, 32–4, 37, 60
United Friendly Boiler Makers' Society *see* Boilermakers
United Irish League 51
United Irishmen xiv
United Operative Plumbers and Domestic Engineers 48
United Society of Boiler Makers and Iron (and Steel) Shipbuilders *see* Boilermakers
United Tyne and District Labourers' Association 4
unskilled workers xiii, 3–5, 44, 52

Urban District Councils 31, 35

vigilance committees 43–4, 46, 48, 55, 71
Voice of Labour 9, 28–30, 79–81, 83, 87–8, 90, 92–3, 96

wages 77–8 *see also* agricultural workers
setting 20–1
Walker, Brian M. 90
Walker, Graham xiv
Walker, William xv, 7, 9, 11–13, 17, 19
Wall, Nicholas 92
Wallace, Revd John Bruce 10, 60–1, 63
War Pensions Committee 35
Watchword of Labour 32, 35–6
Waterford, County xii–xiii, 78–82, 89–93, 95, 97–8
farm strike 83–95
Waterford City Hall 81, 86, 91
Waterford Farmers' Association (WFA) 83–8, 93
Waterford News 90
Waterford Standard 90
Waterford Star 90
Waterford Workers' Council 86–7, 94
Waugh, Robert 18–19
Weir, Bob 26
West Belfast Unionist Club 44
Westminster Gazette 44–5, 60
White, Jack 95
White, Vincent 89, 92
White Cross 47, 73–4
'White Guardism' 91, 93
Whitley, Henry 18
Wilson, Alec 33, 35
Women's International League 39, 56
women's rights 7
Workers' Bulletin 20, 23–4, 26–8, 30
Workers' Republic 79, 93–4
Workers' Union 53, 70–1
Workman, Clark 2, 41, 44, 48, 54
Wright (Baird), Margaret 1